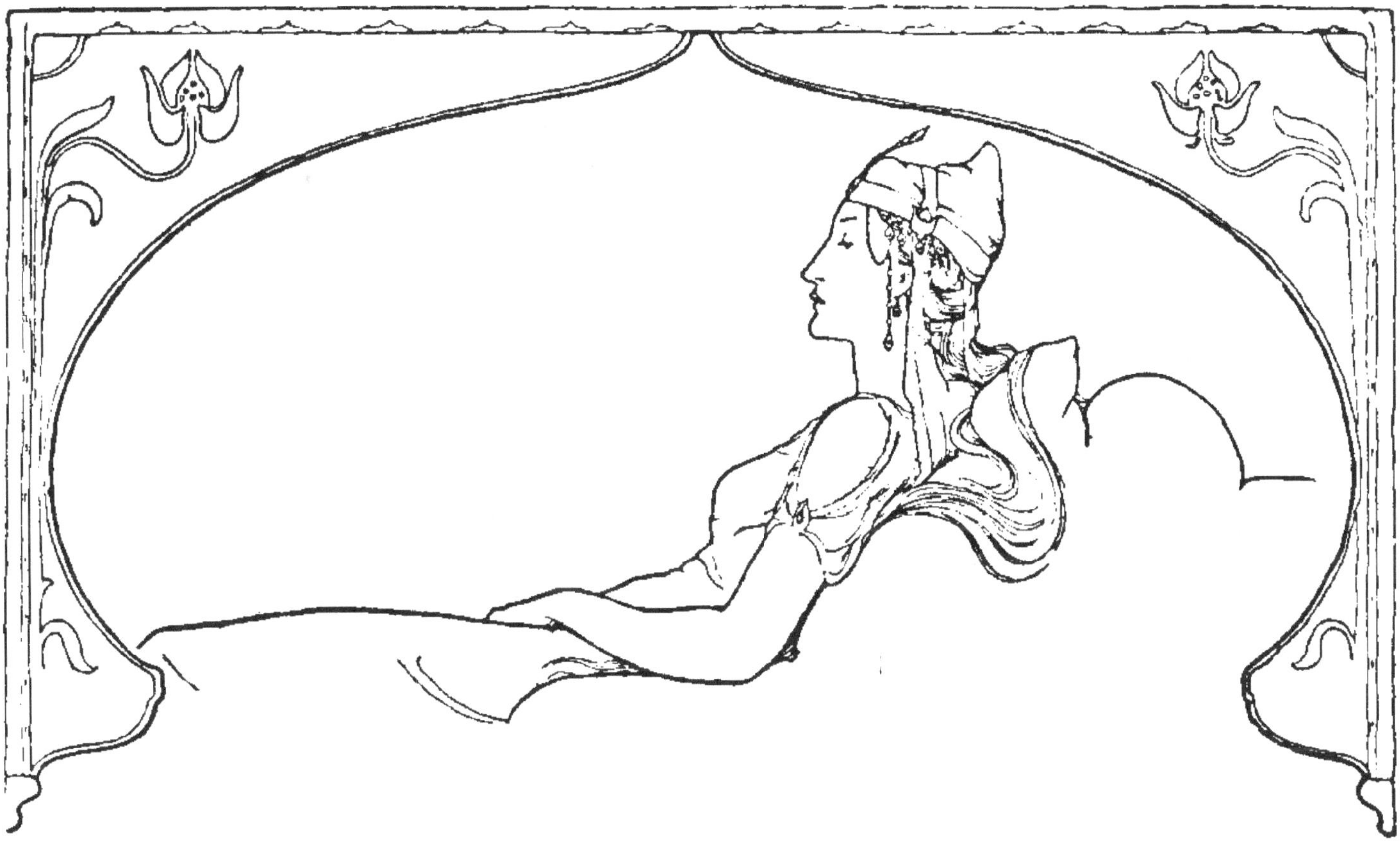

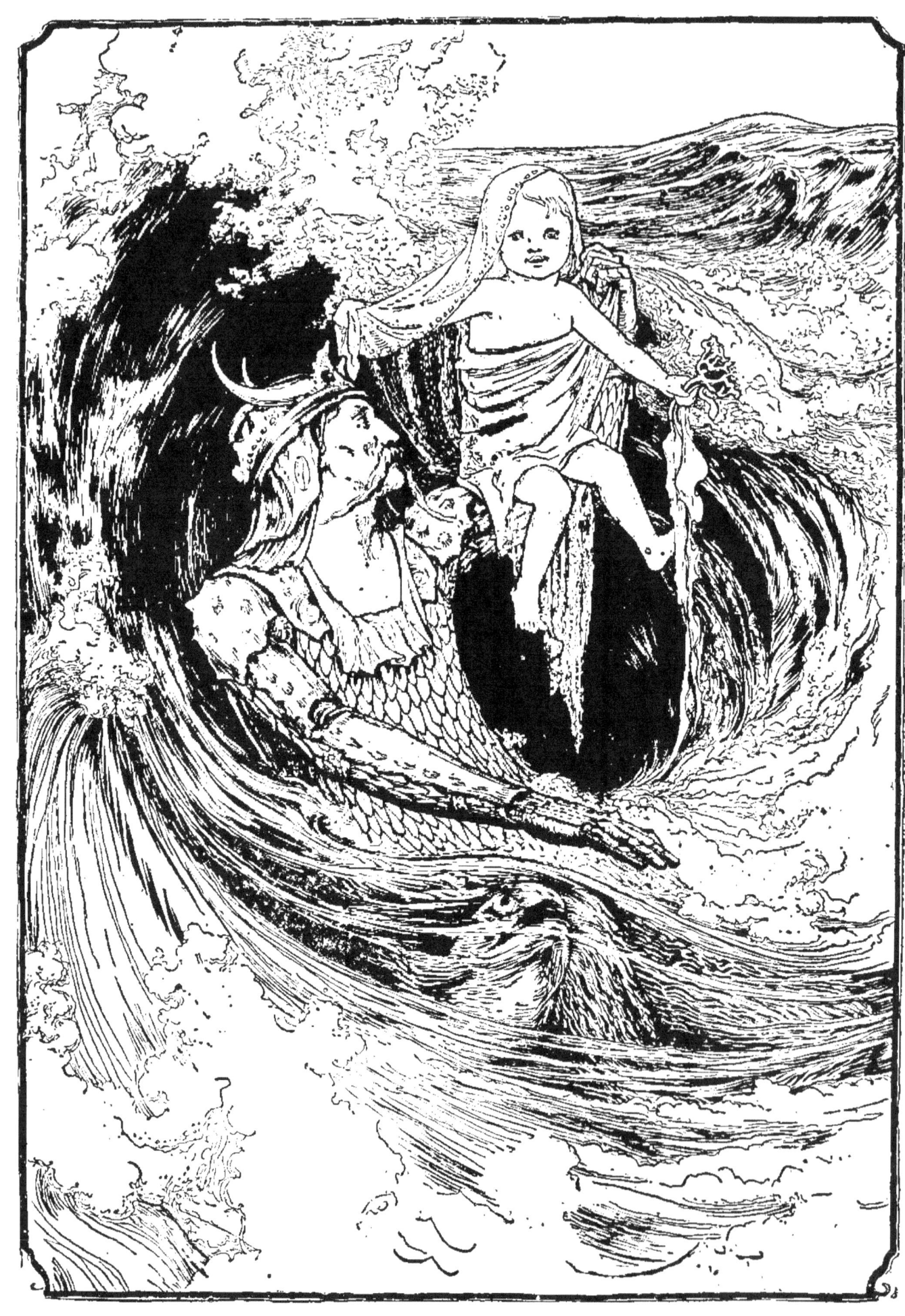

KING SALEH AND PRINCE BEDER

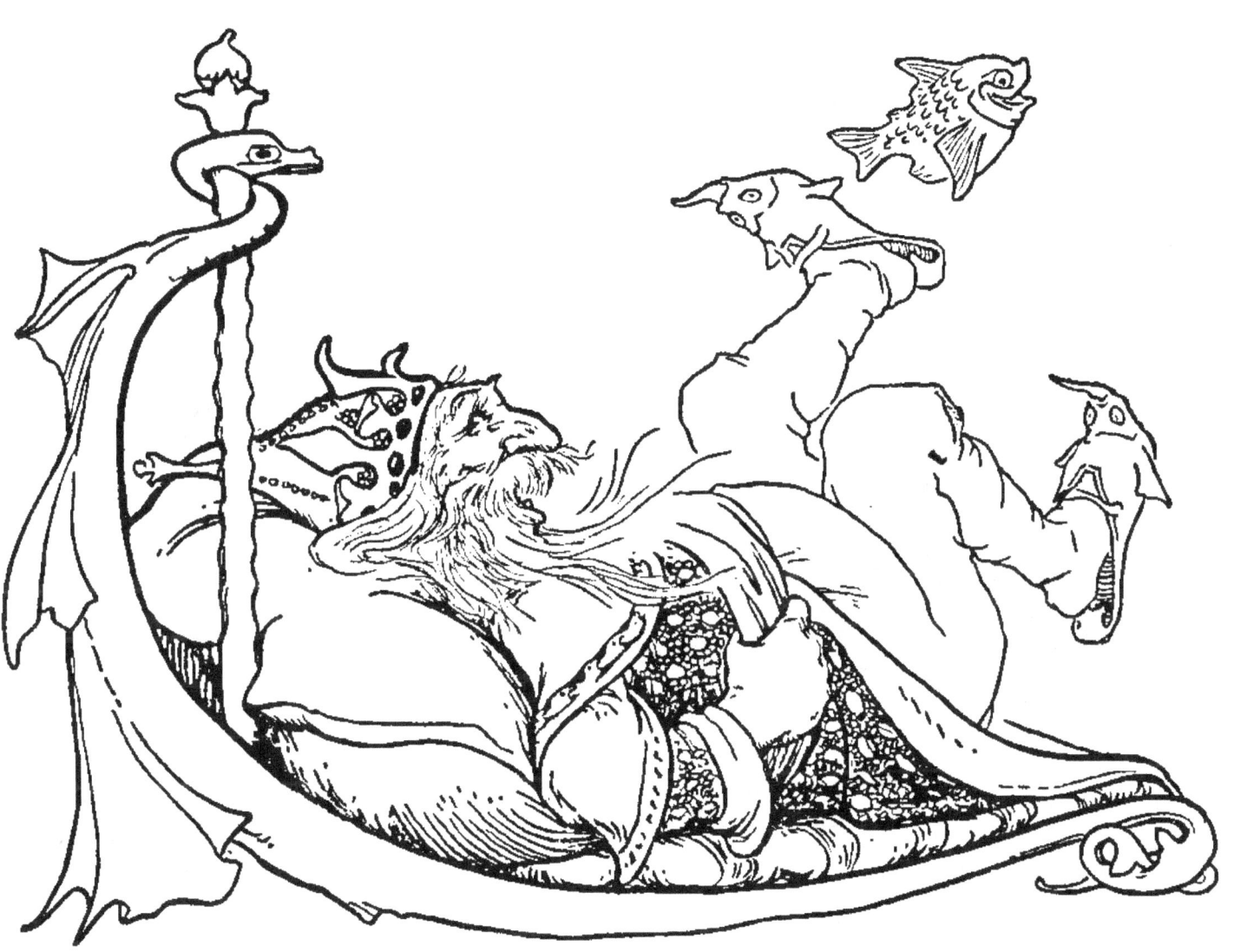

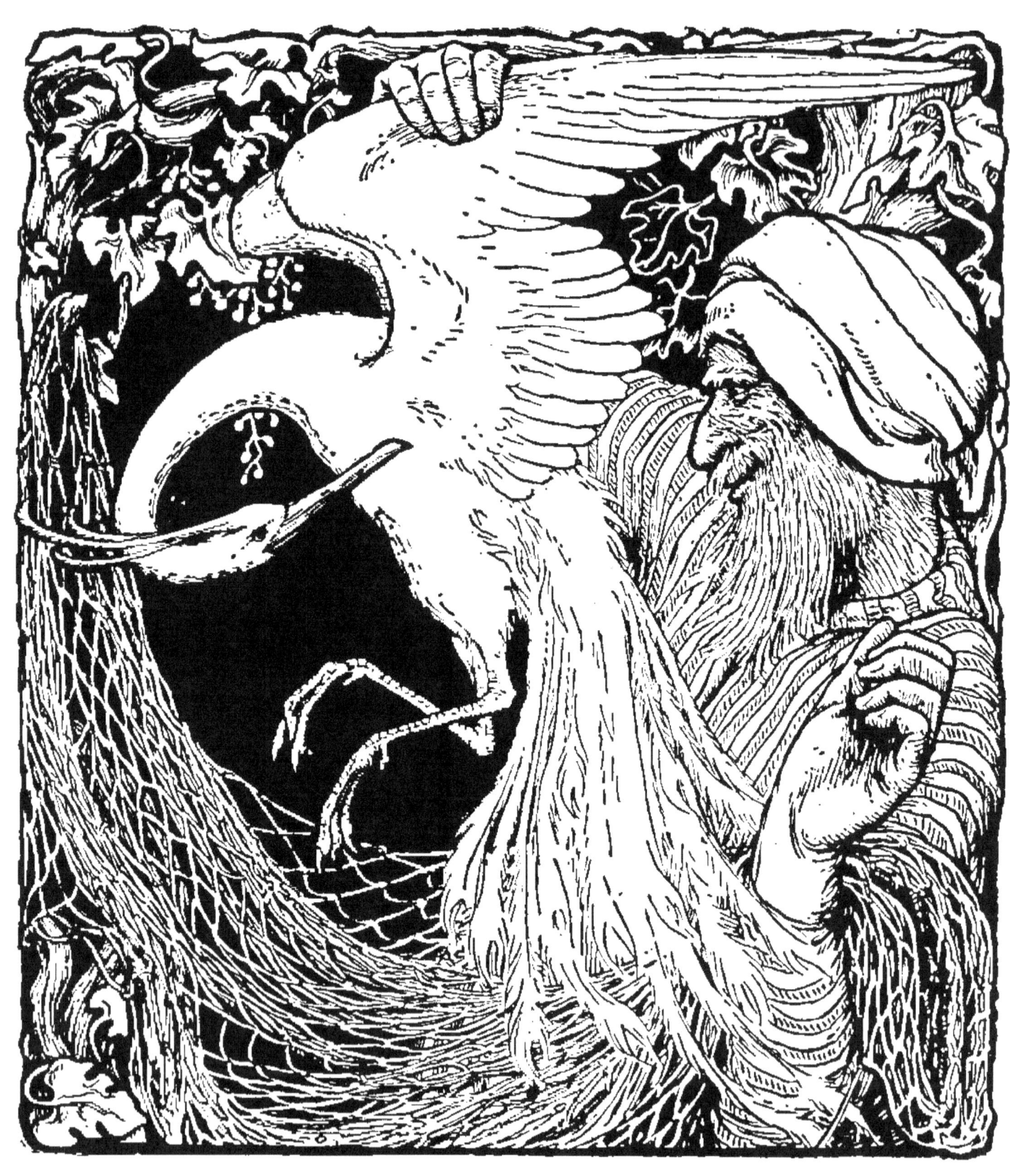

THE WHITE BIRD

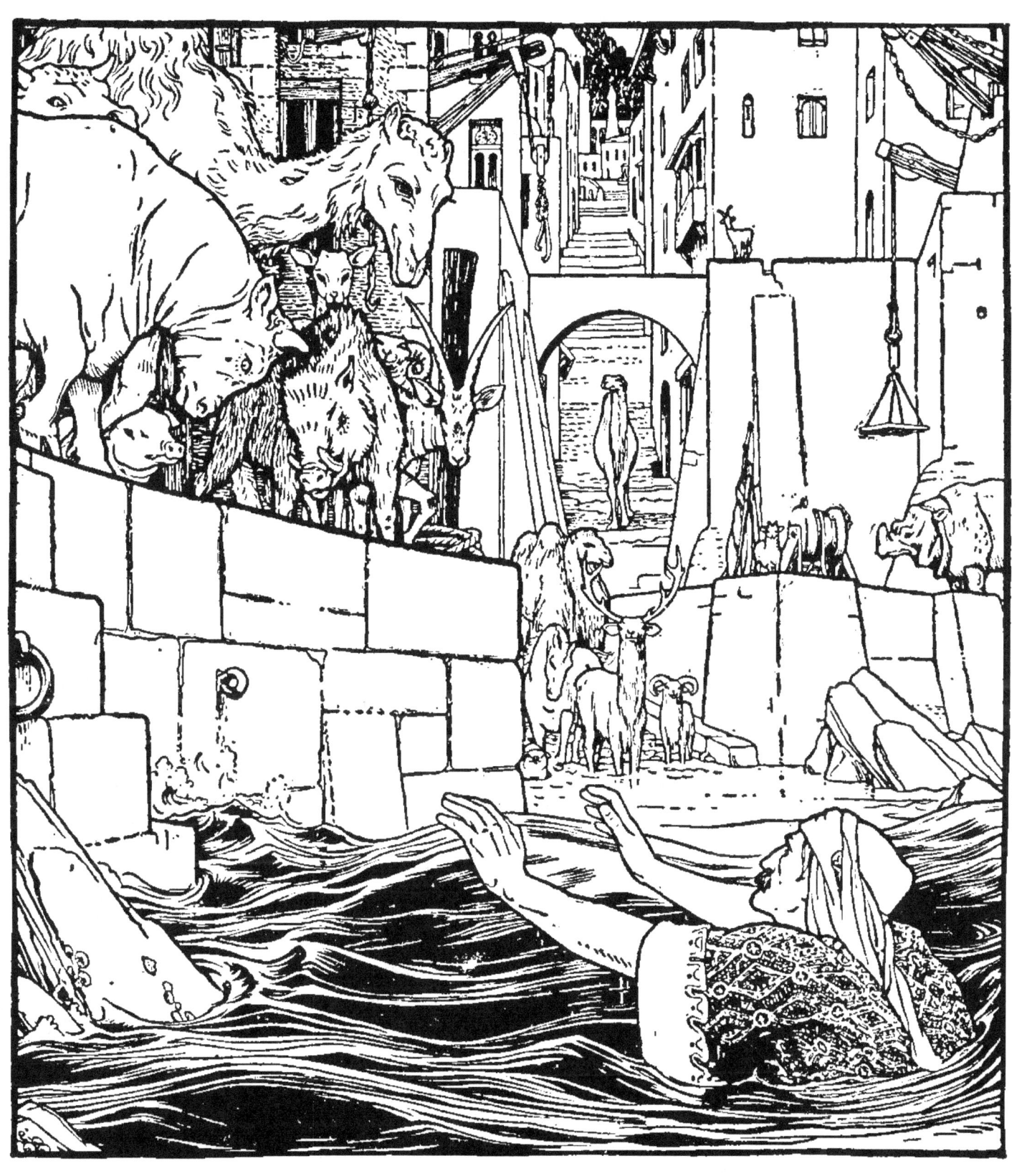

THE ANIMALS OPPOSE KING BEDER'S LANDING

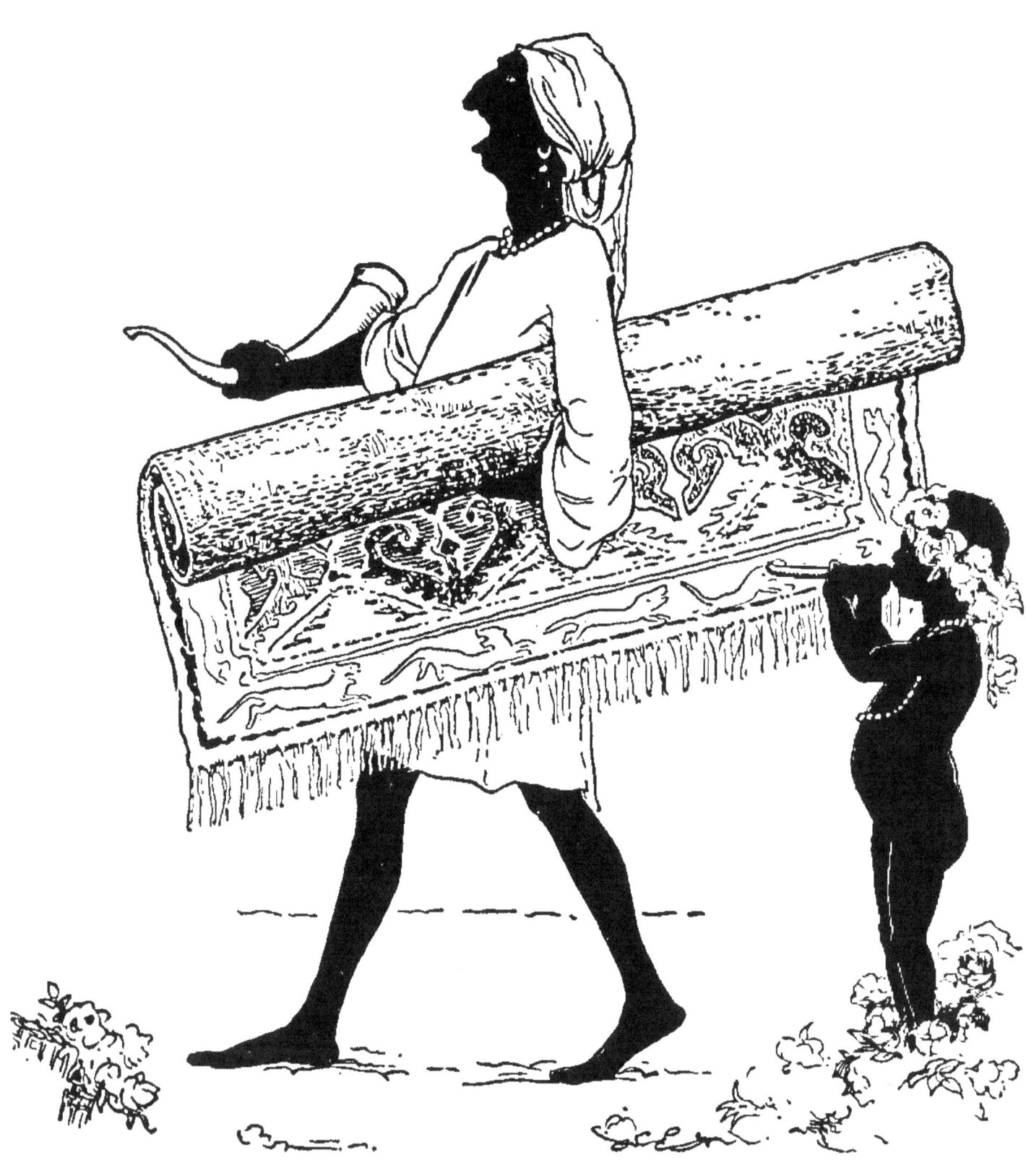

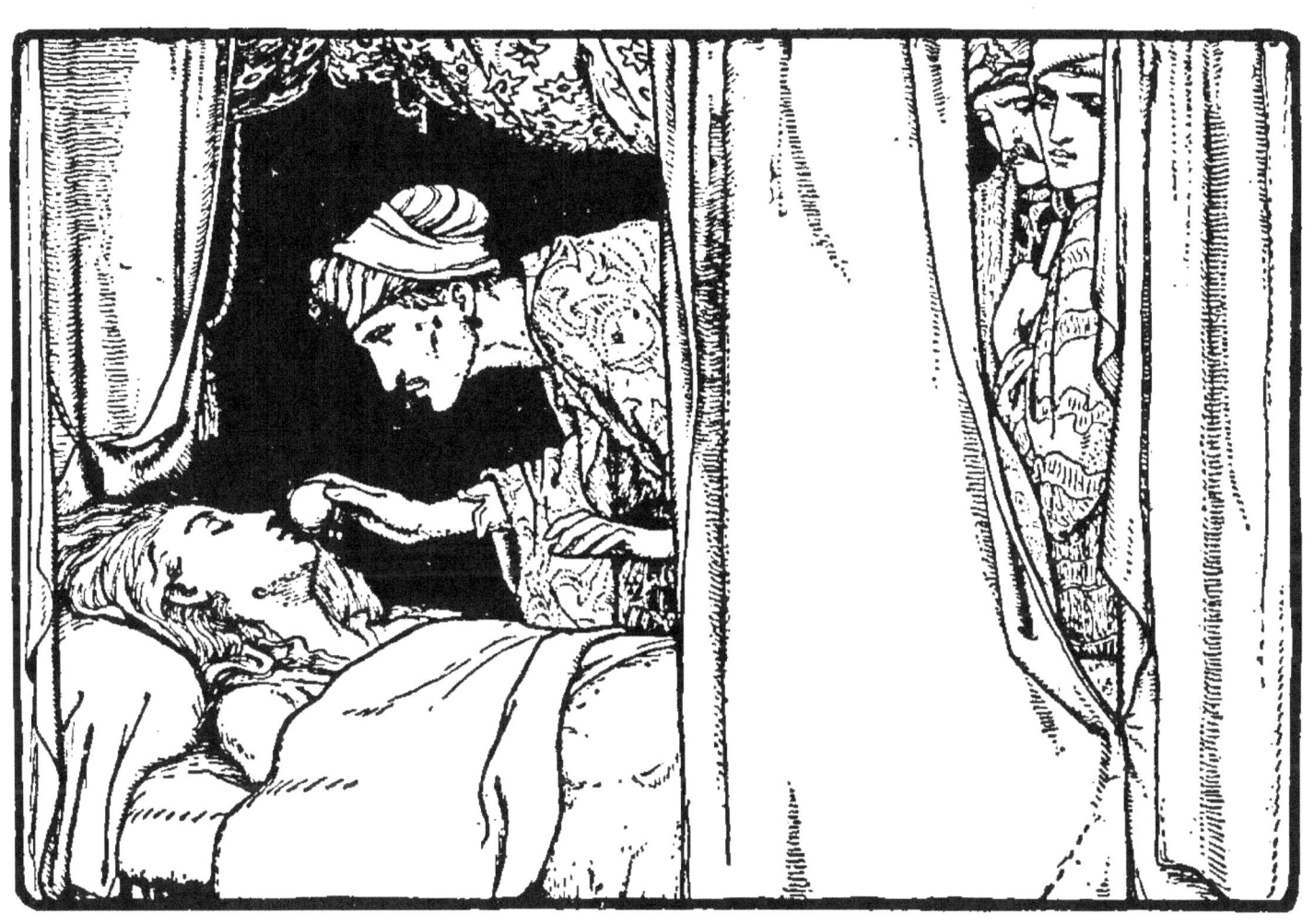

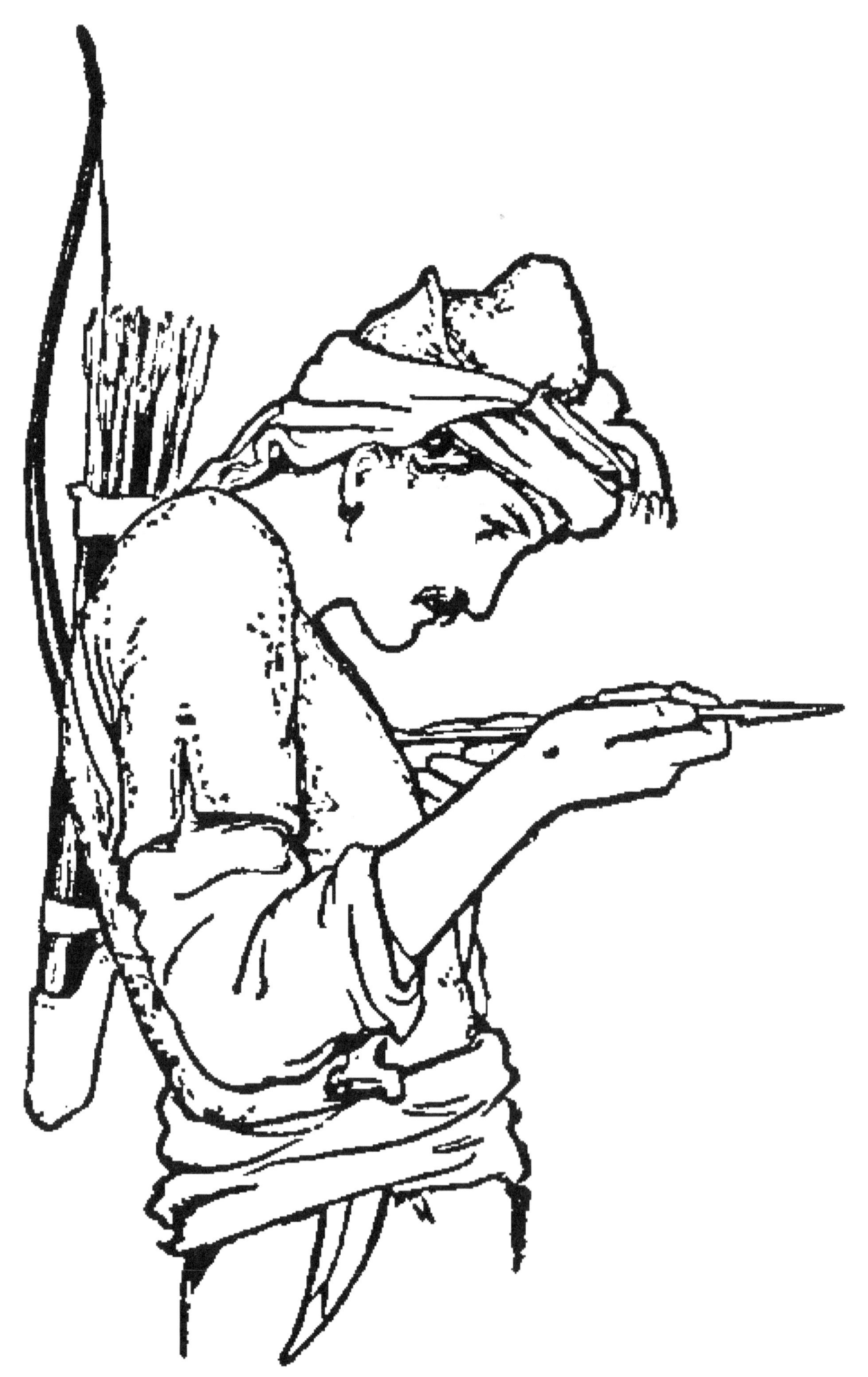

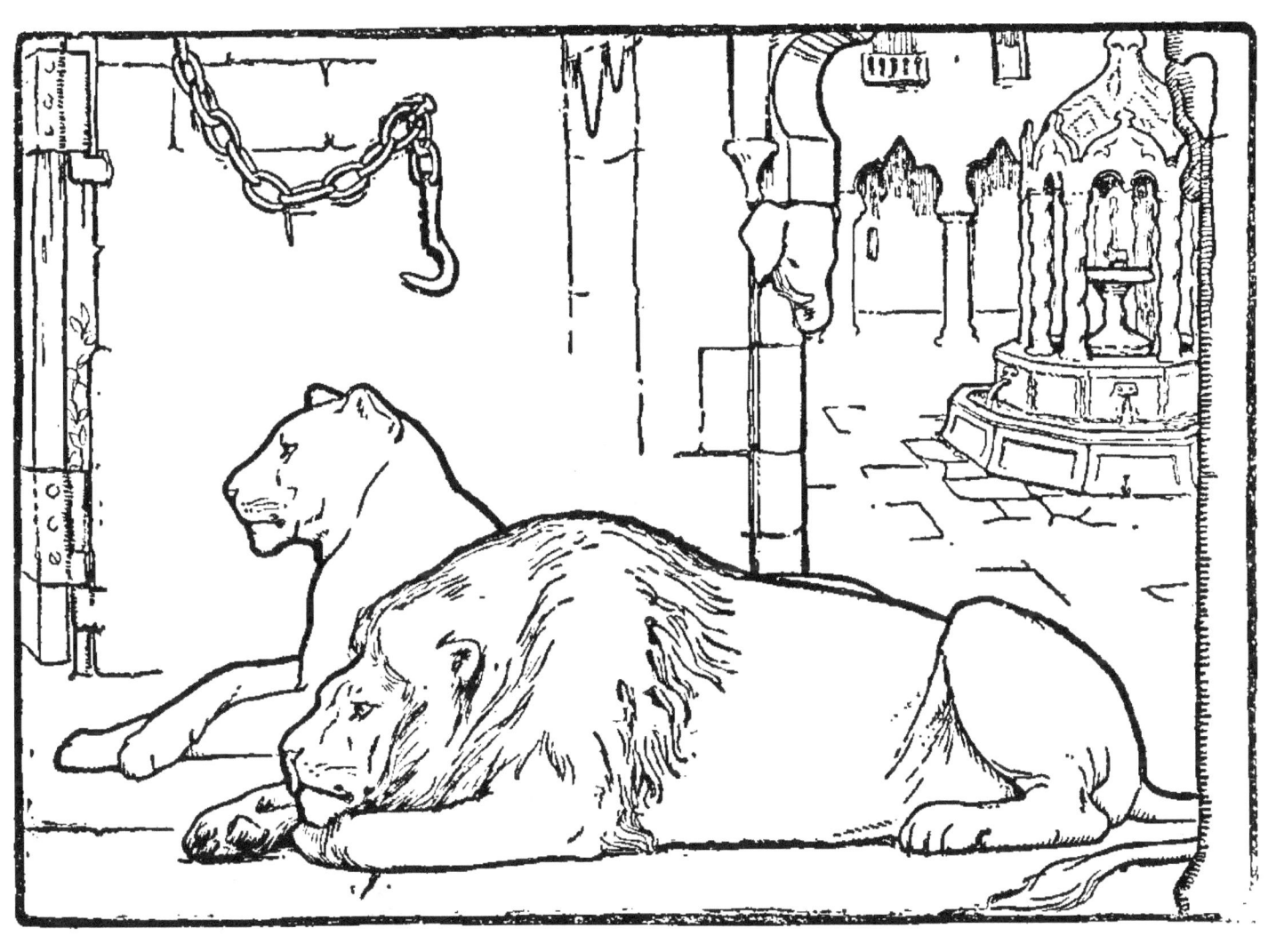

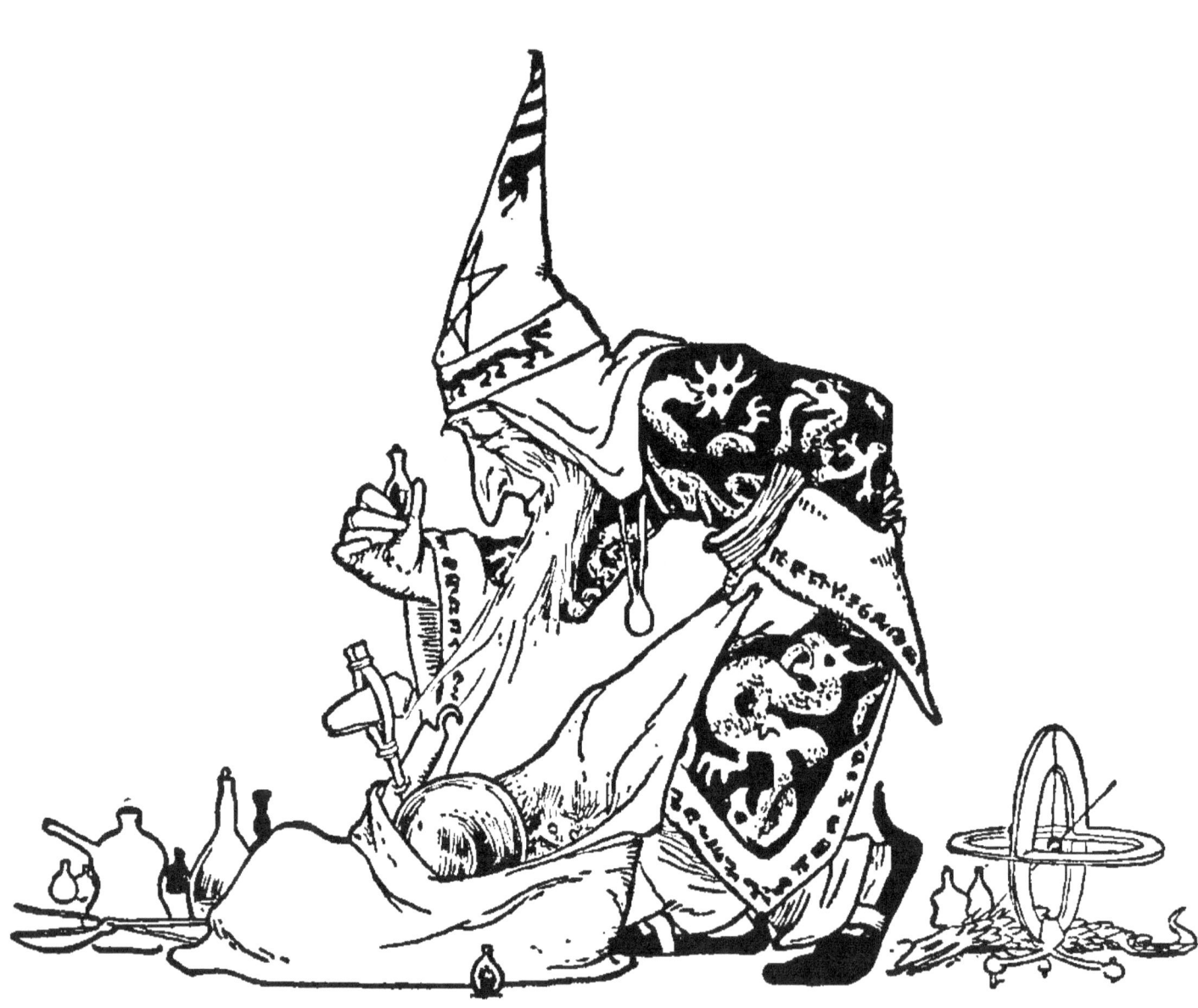

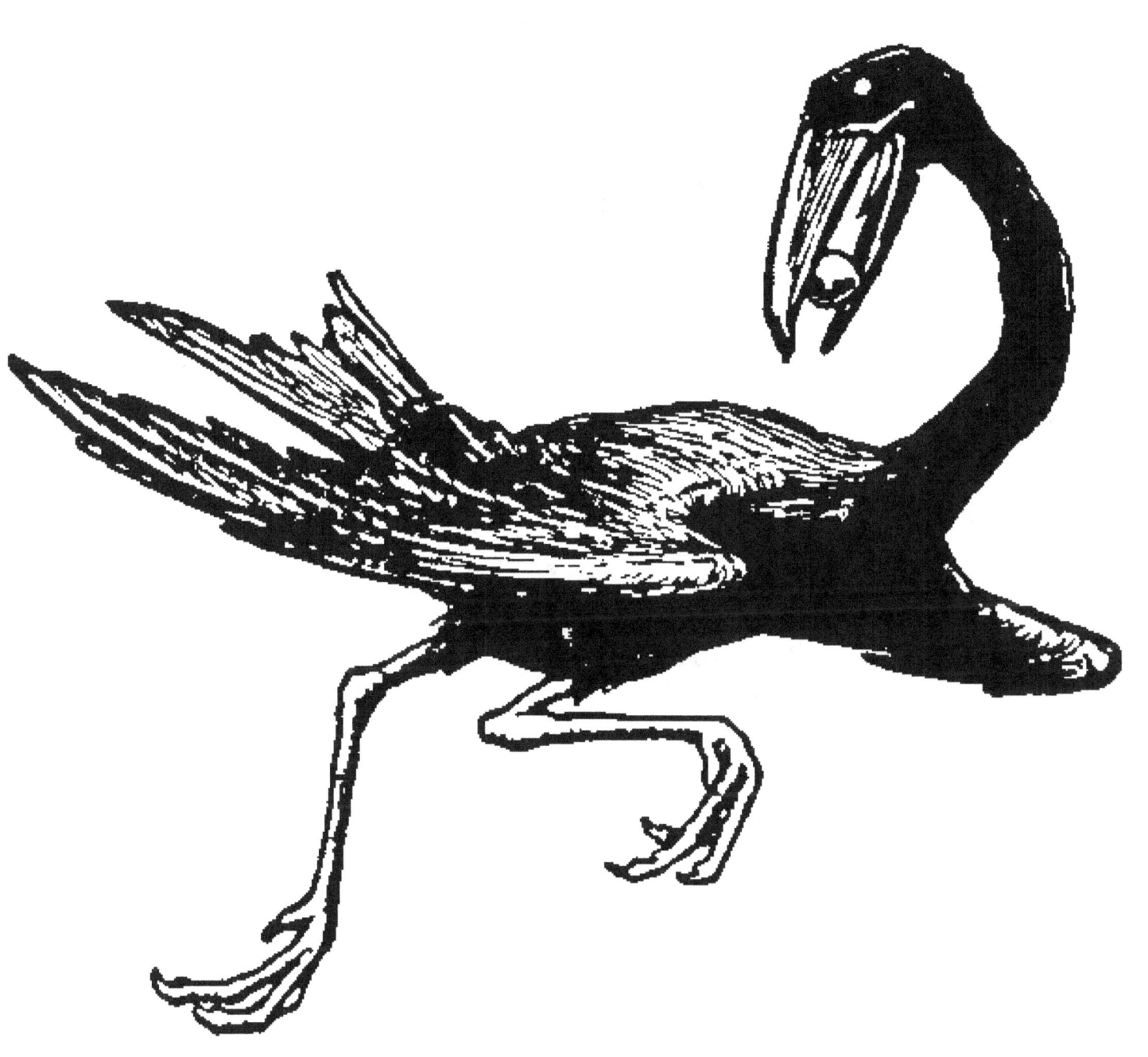

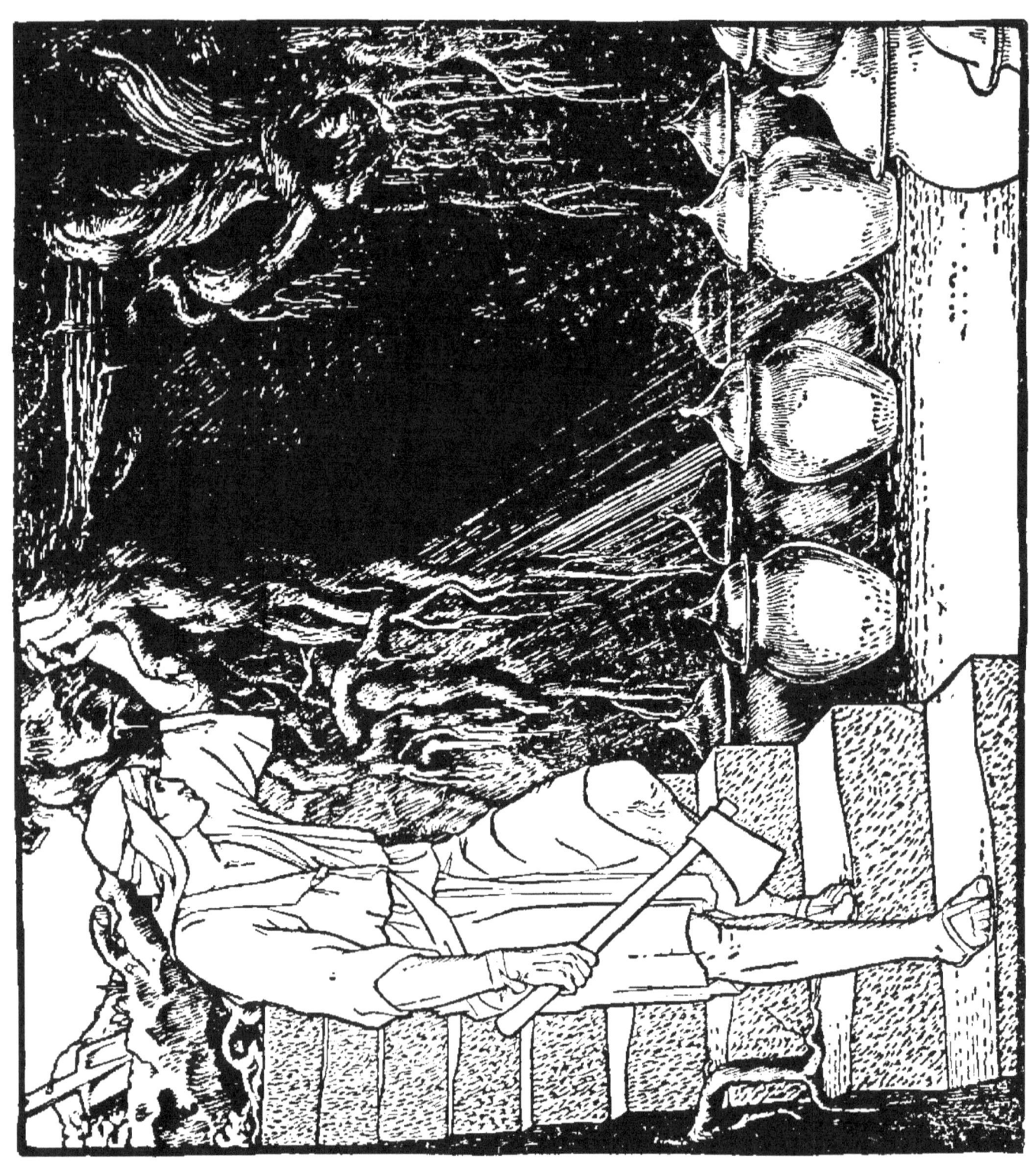

CAMARALZAMAN AND THE BRASS URNS

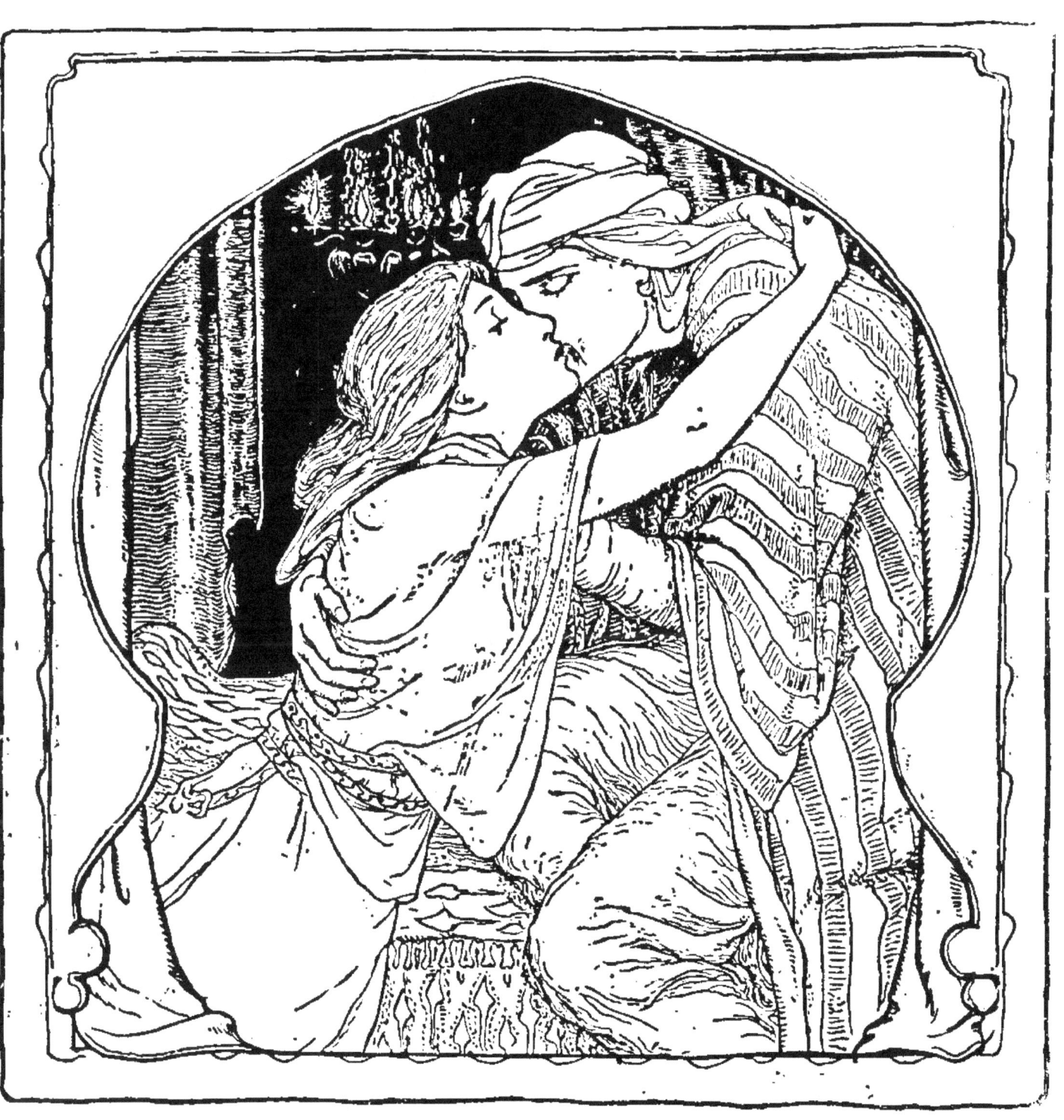

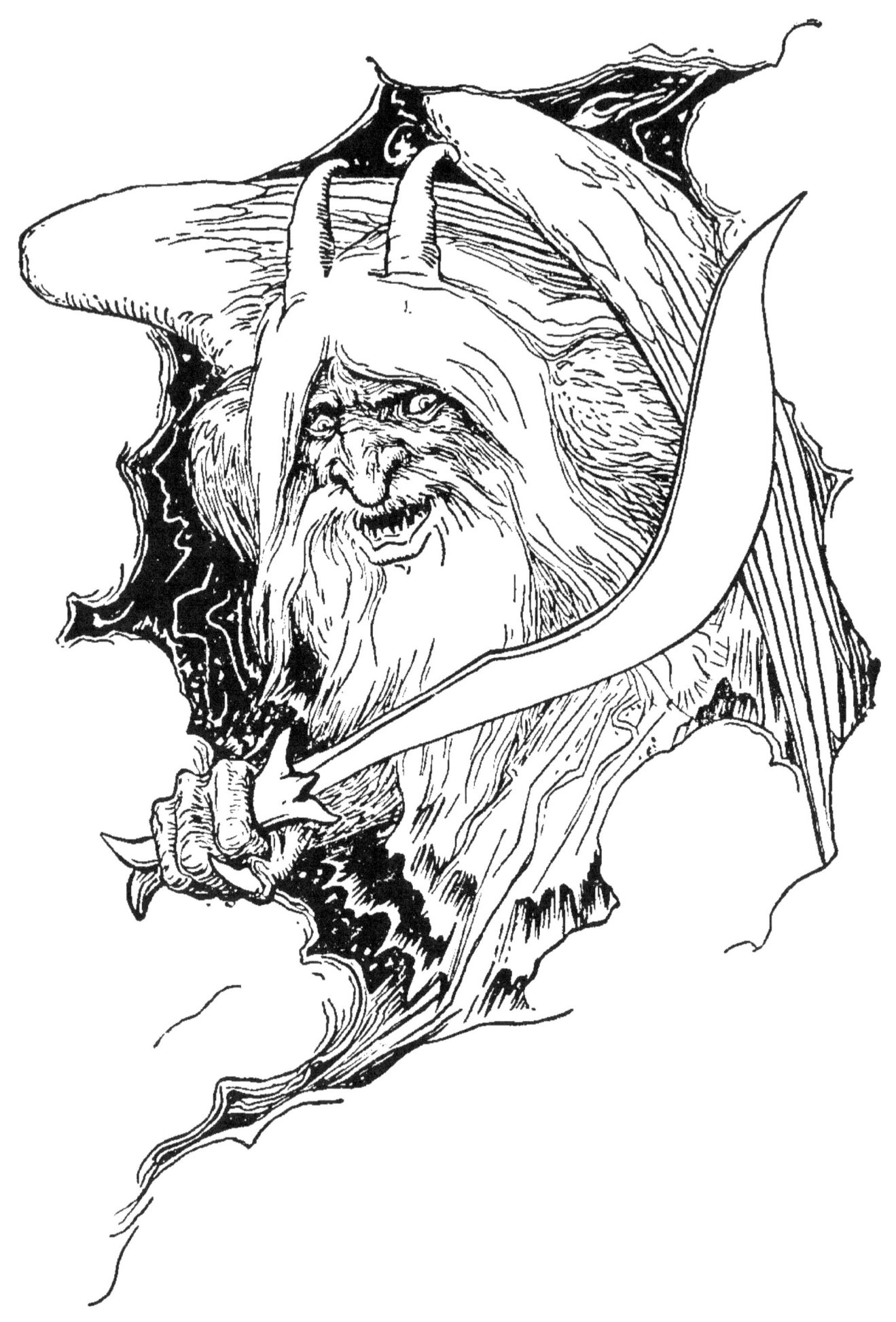

The enchanted palace opened, and made a passage for the genie

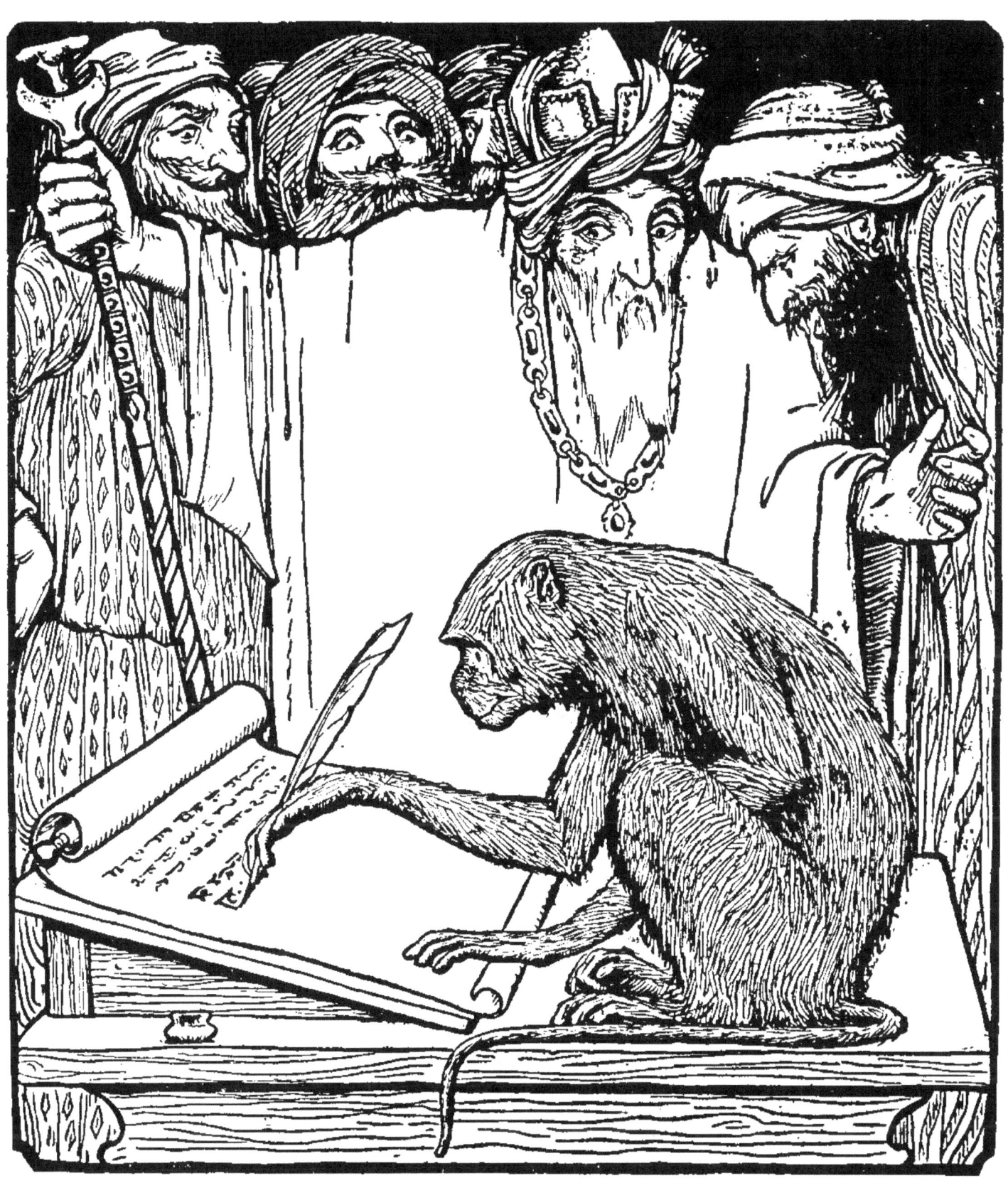

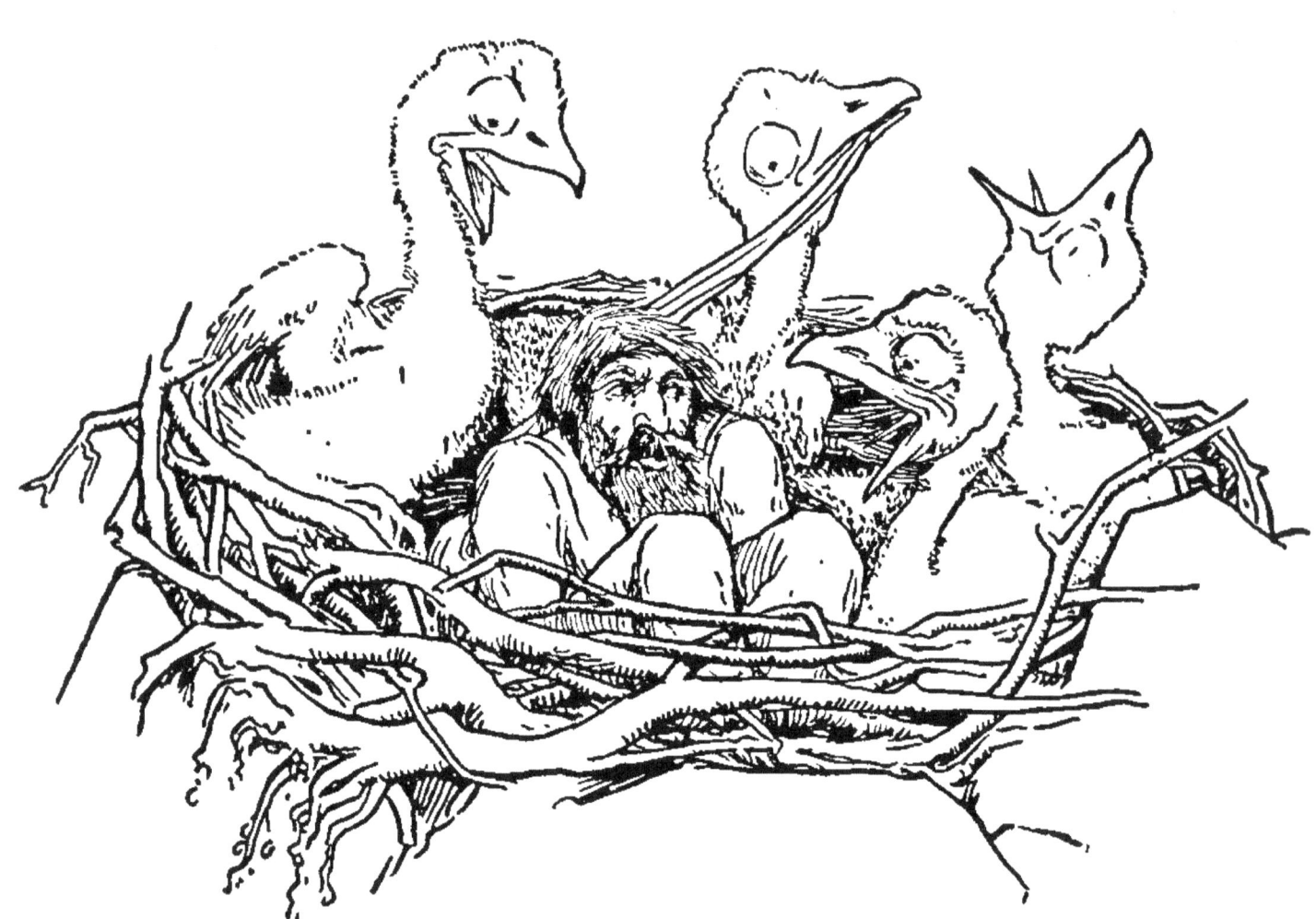

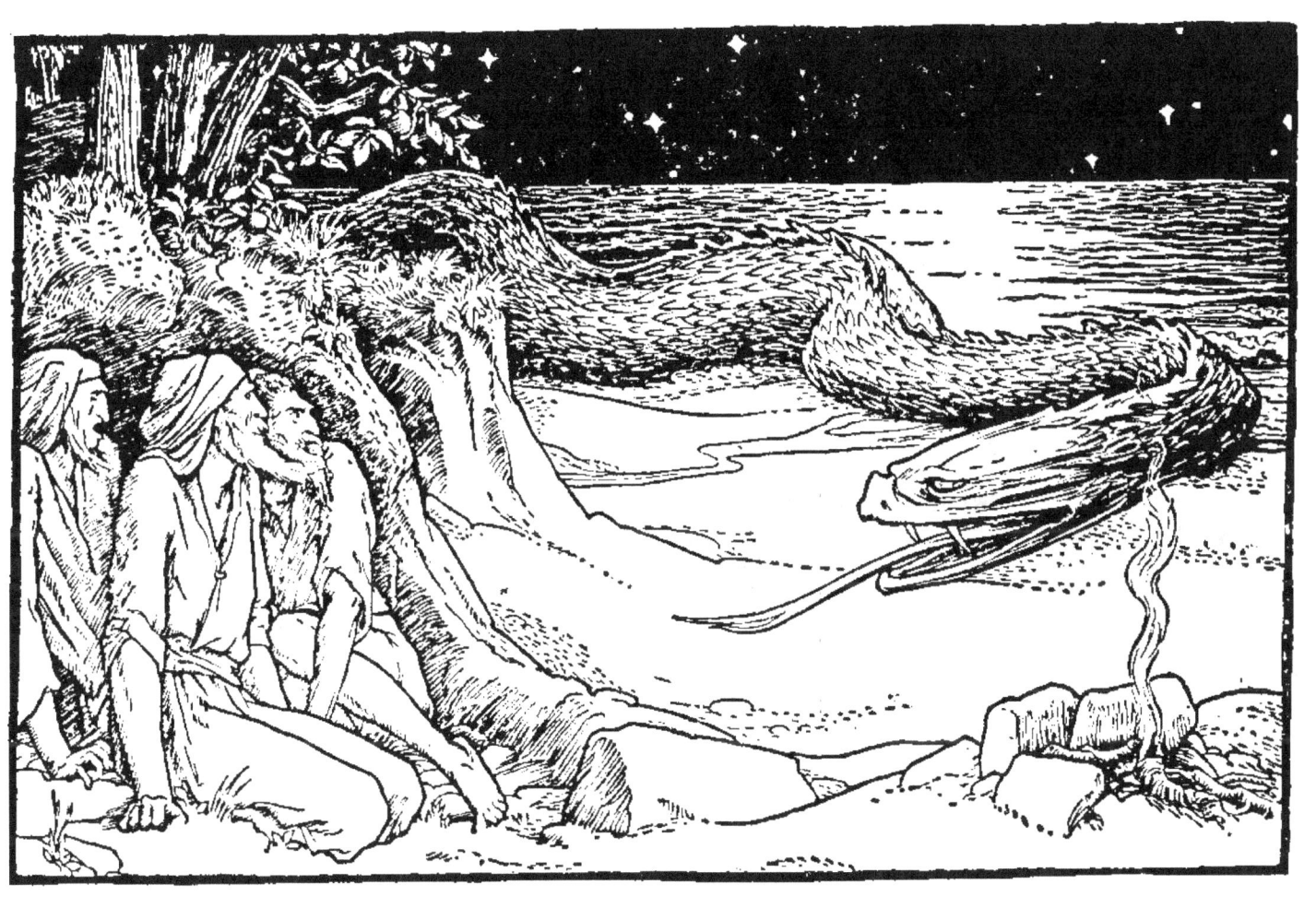

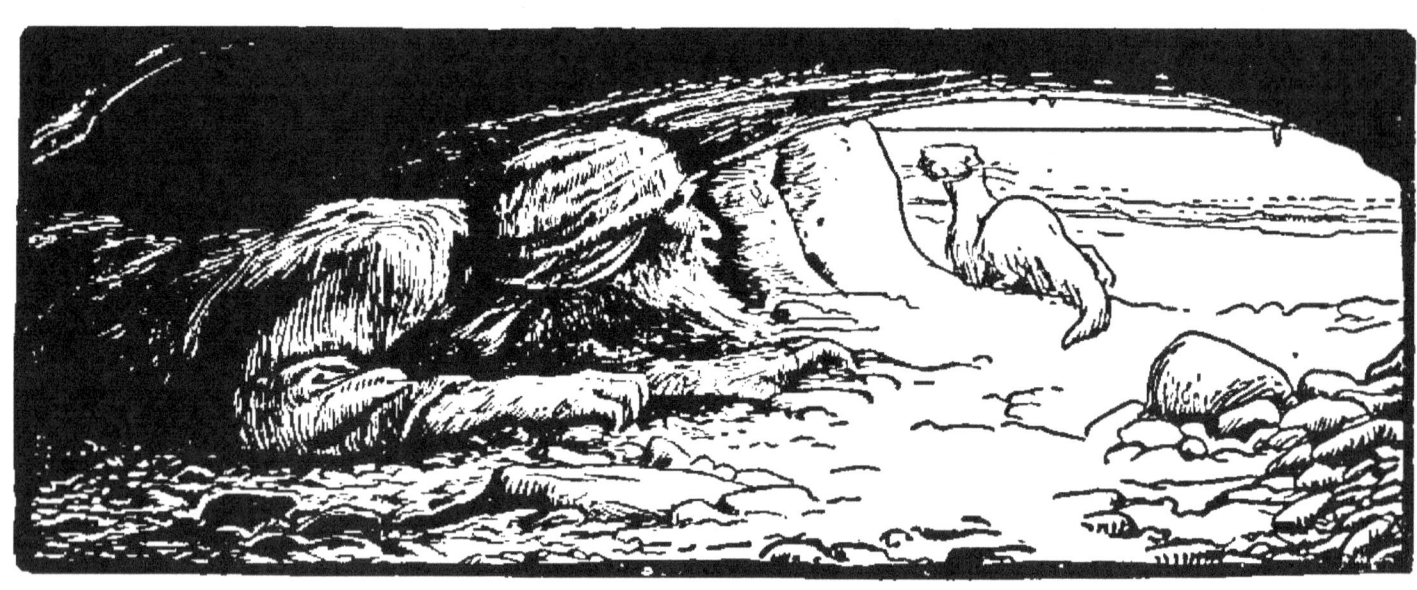

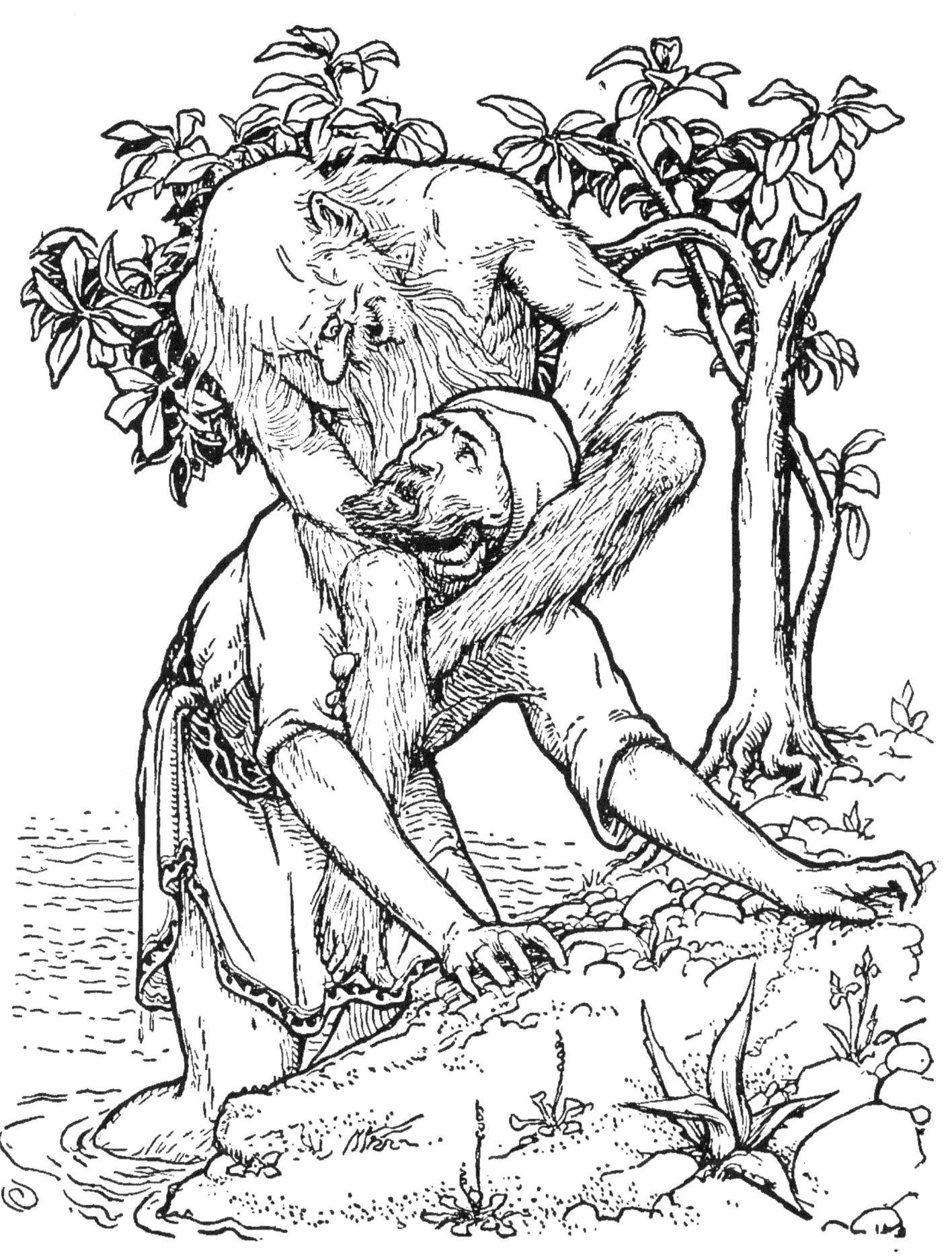

SINBAD AND THE OLD MAN OF THE SEA

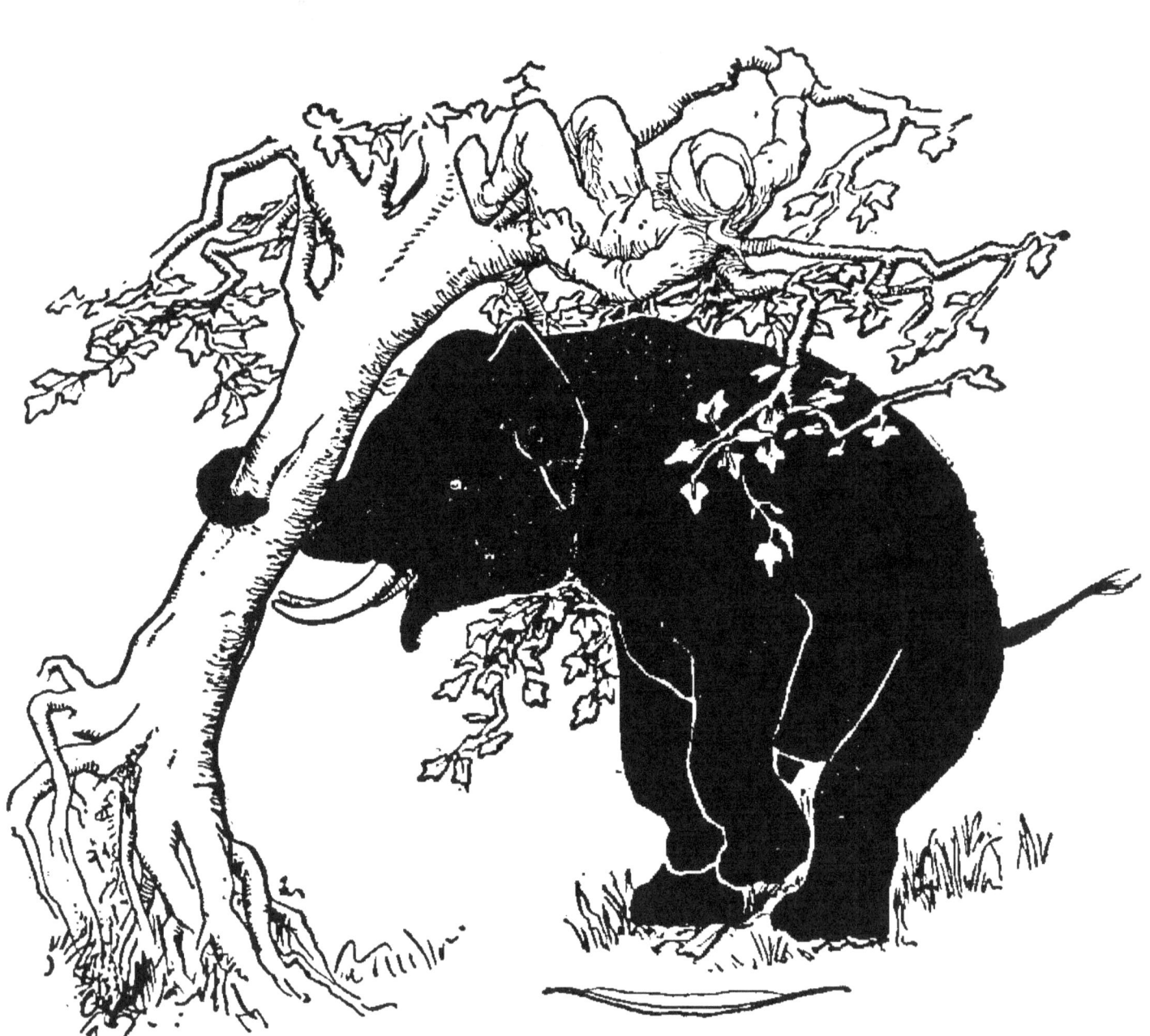

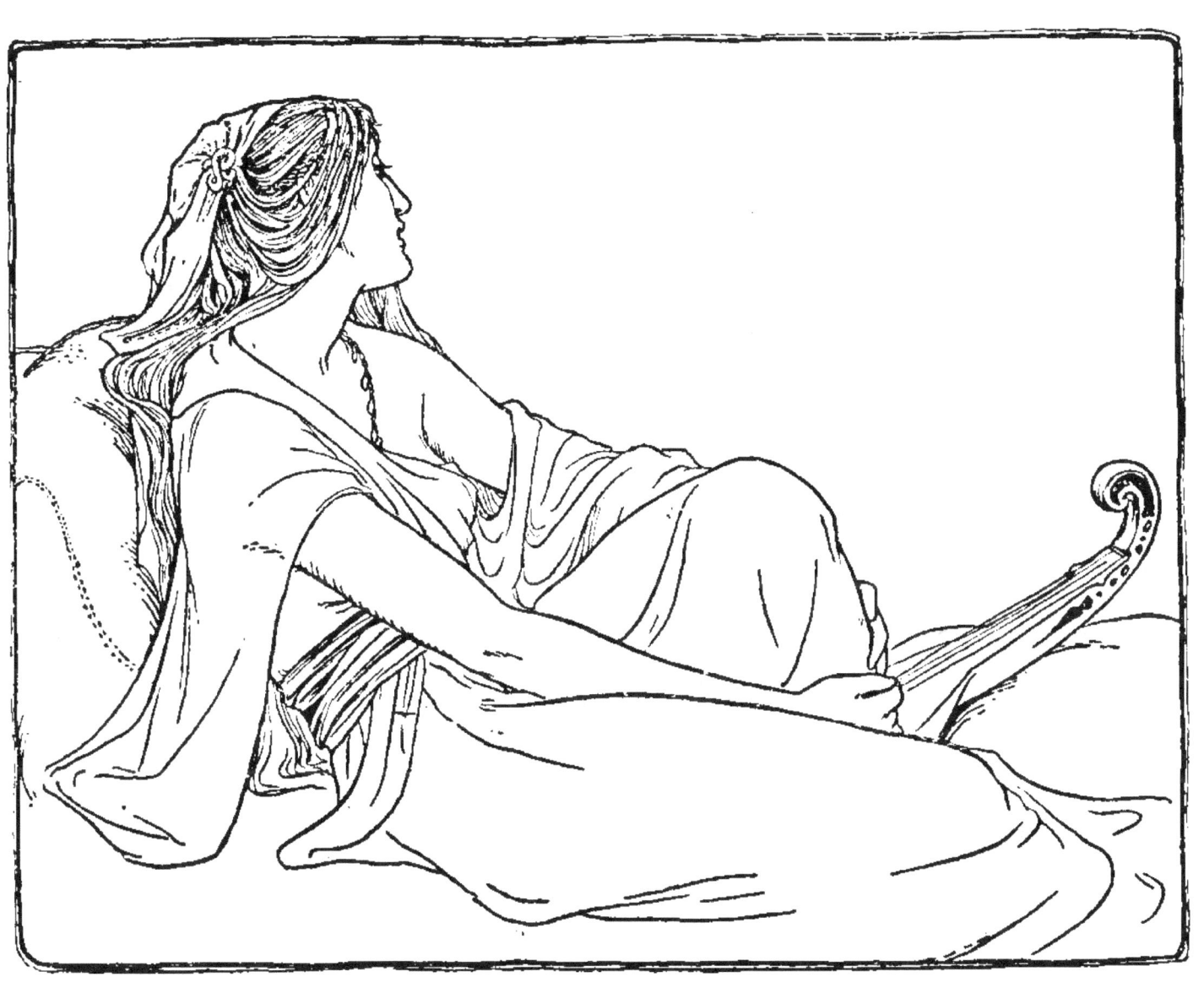

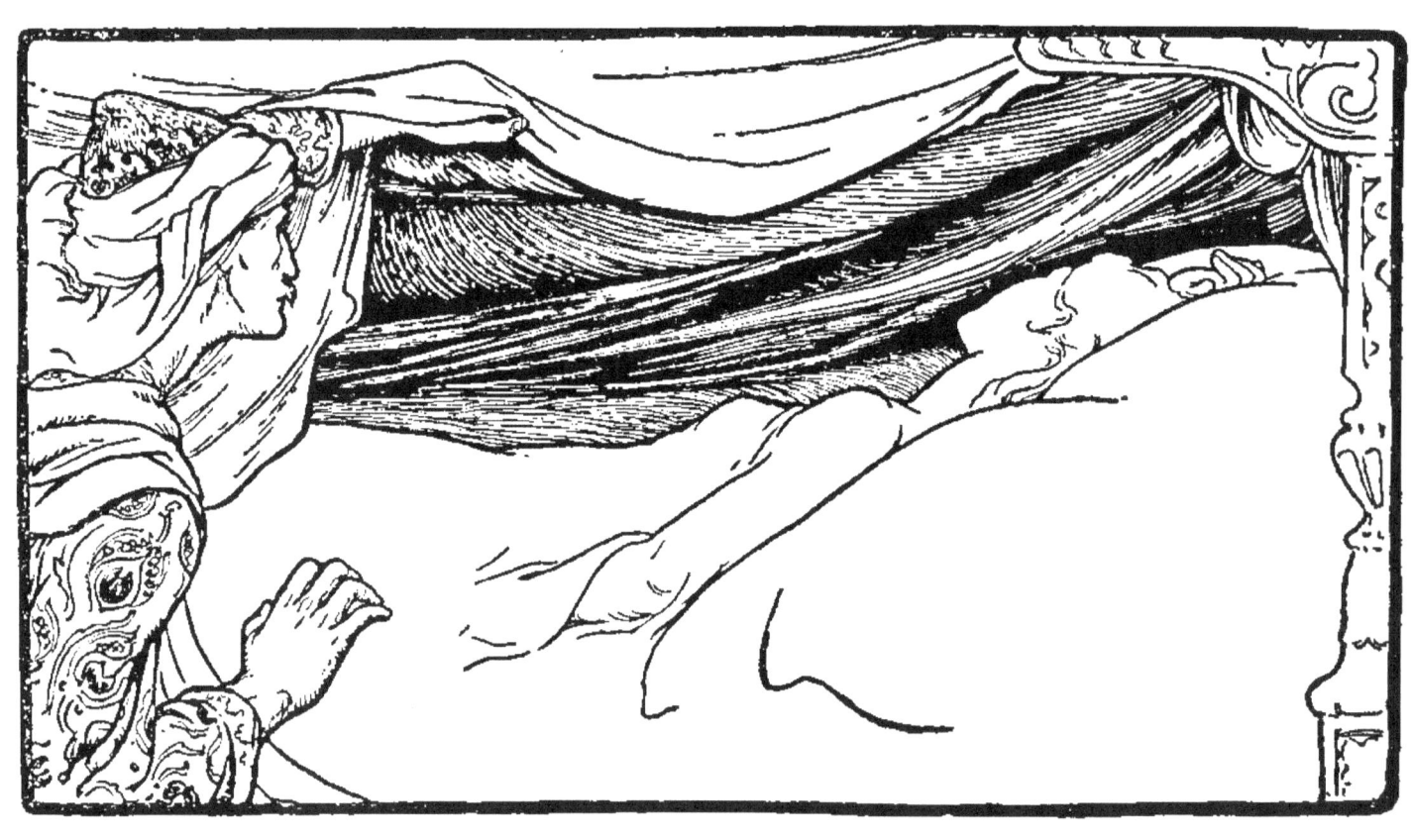

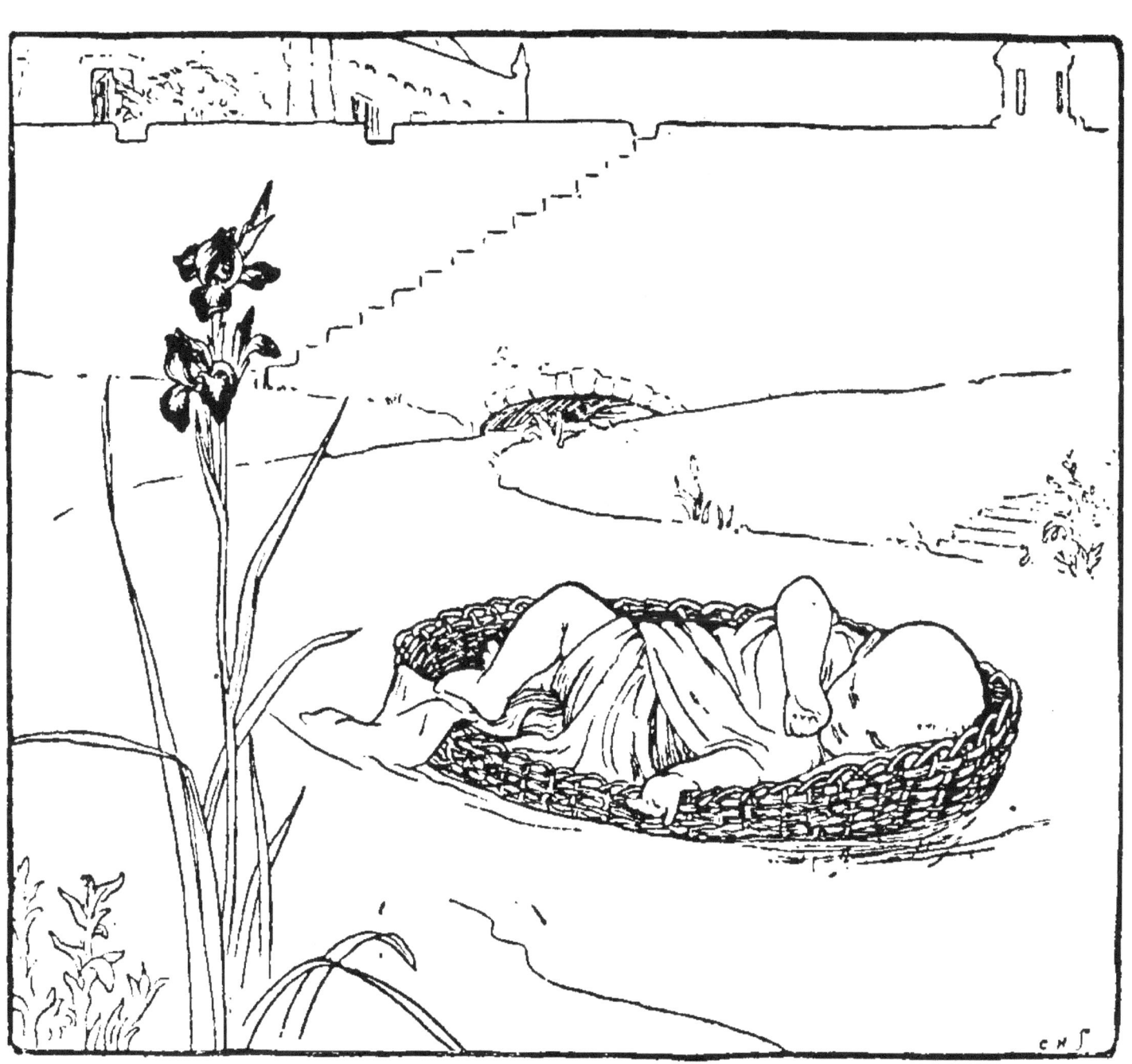

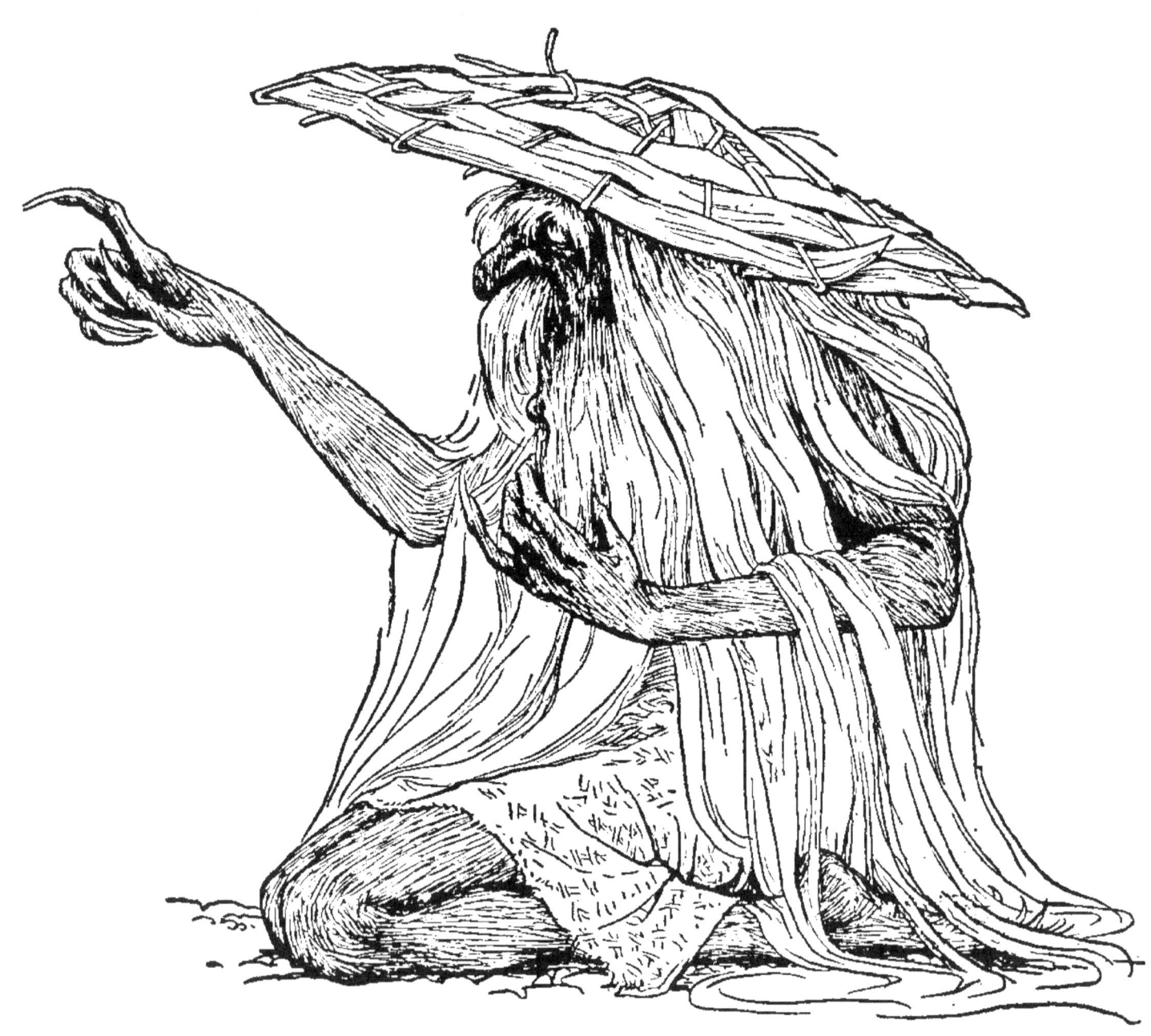

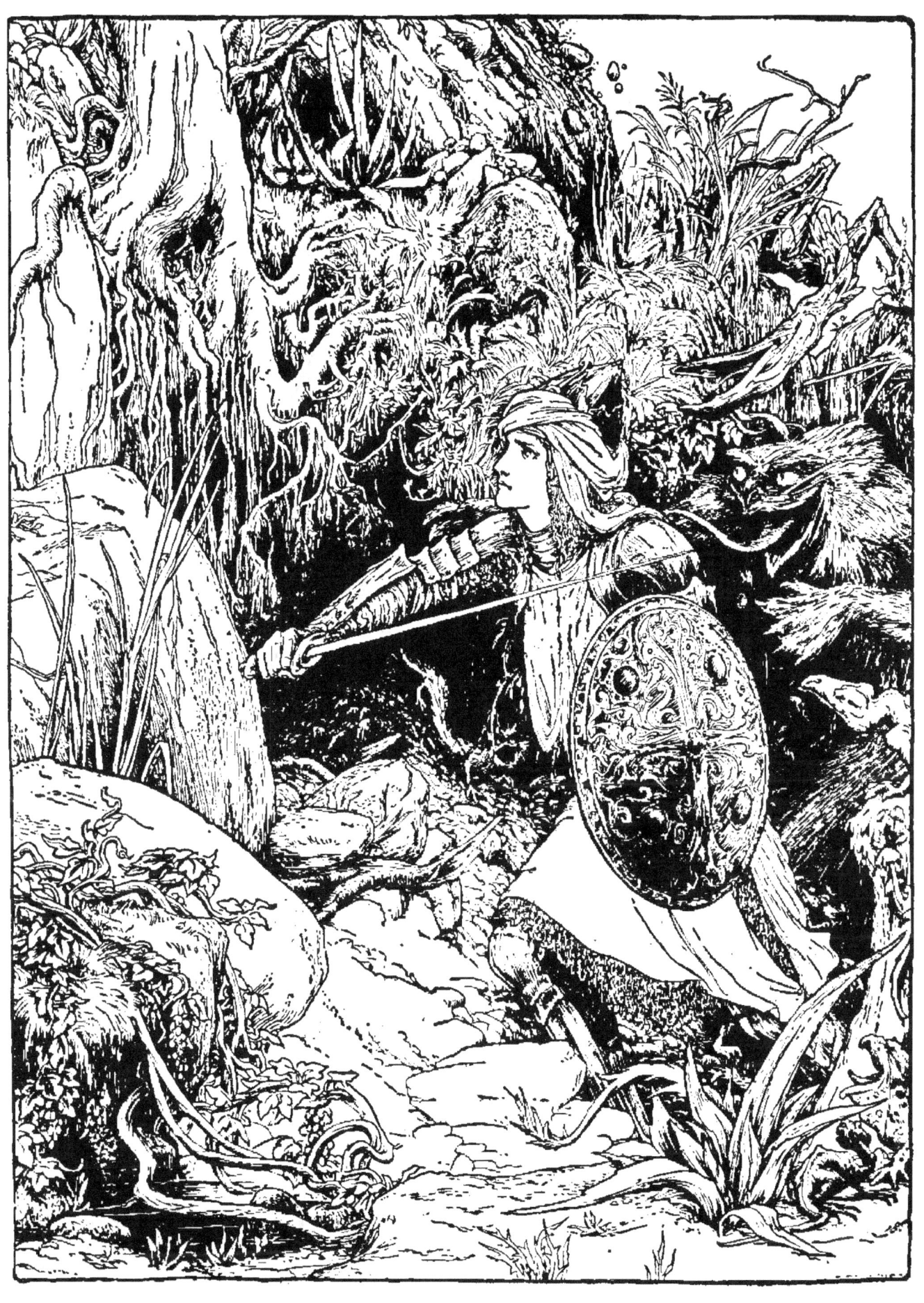

LOOK·NOT·BACK
PARIZADE

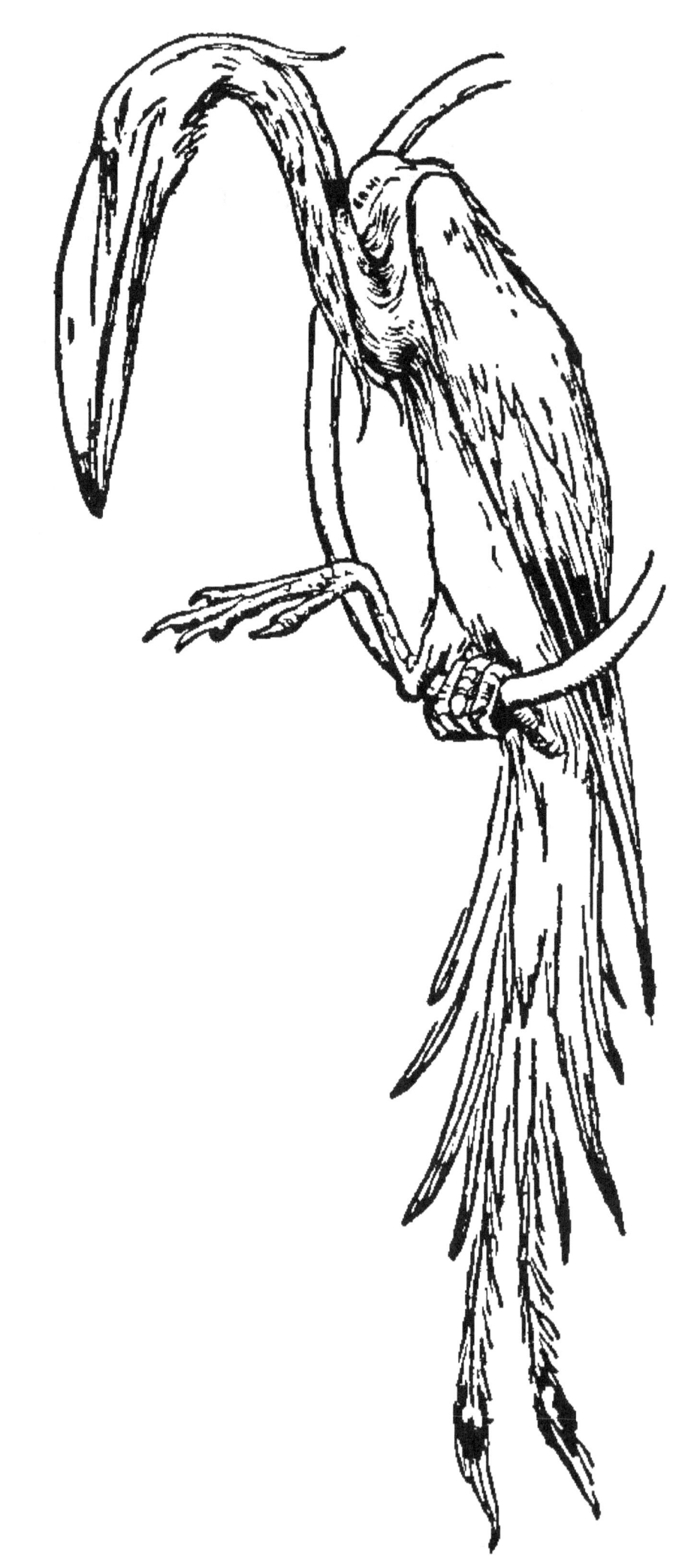

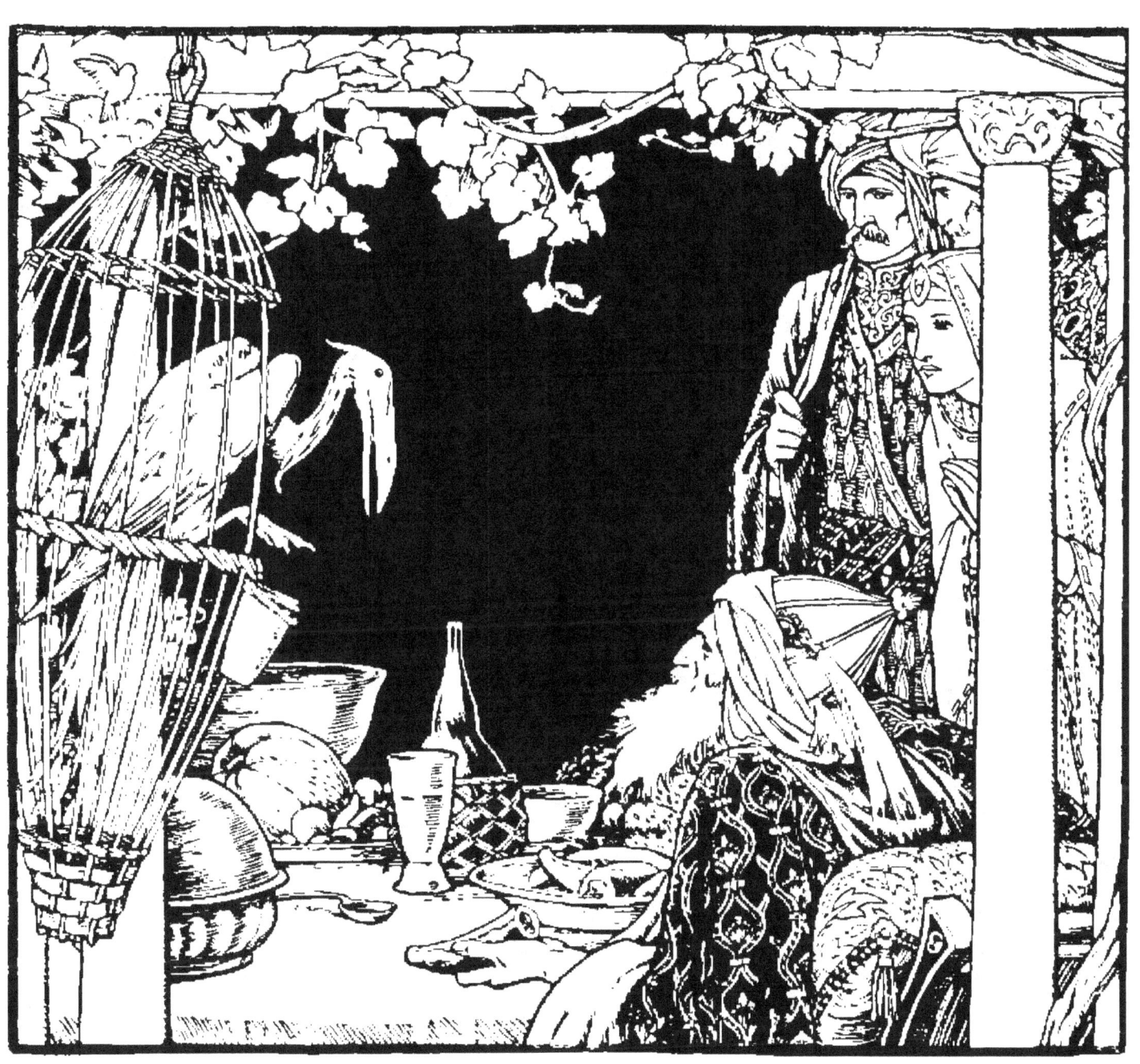

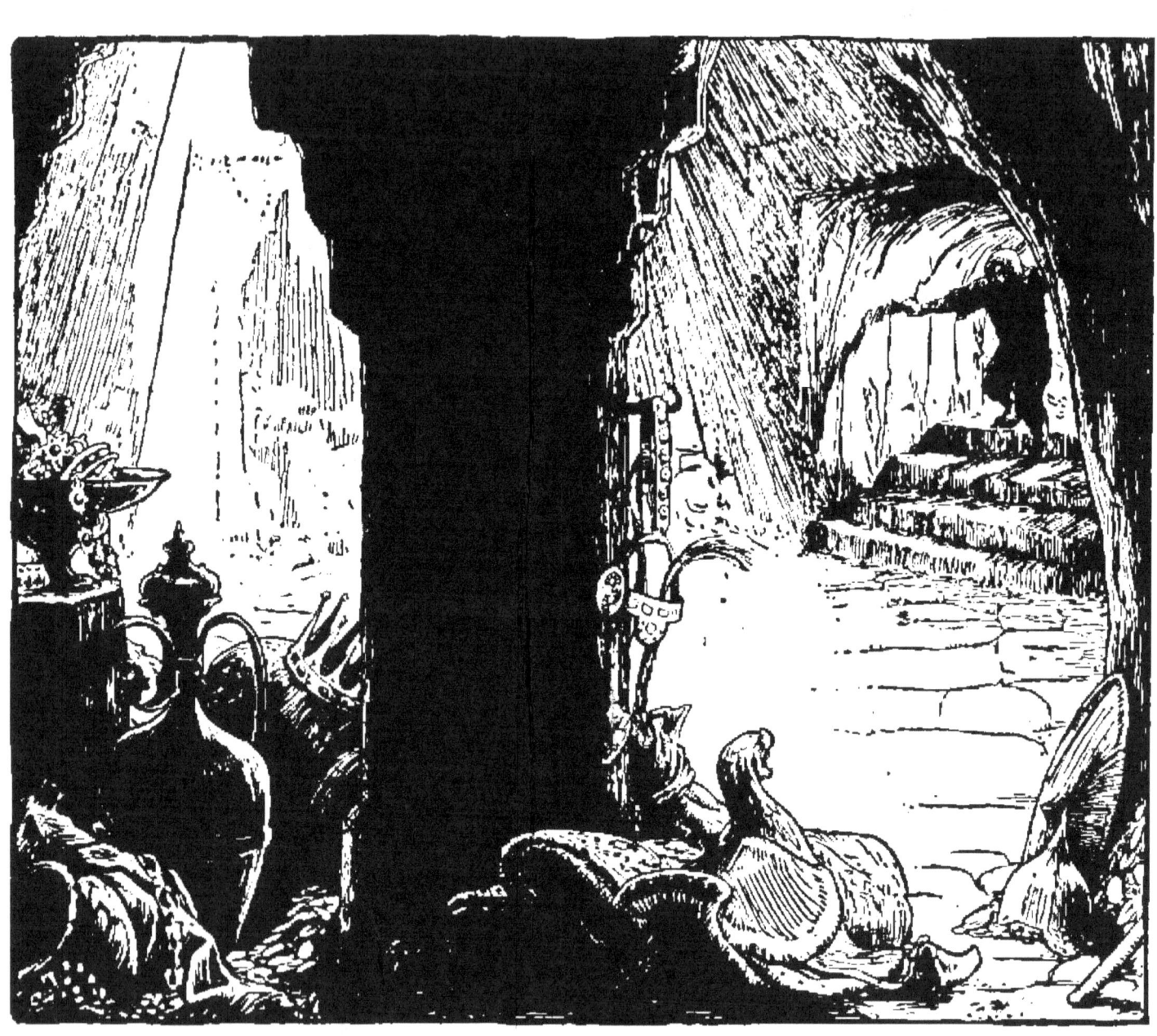

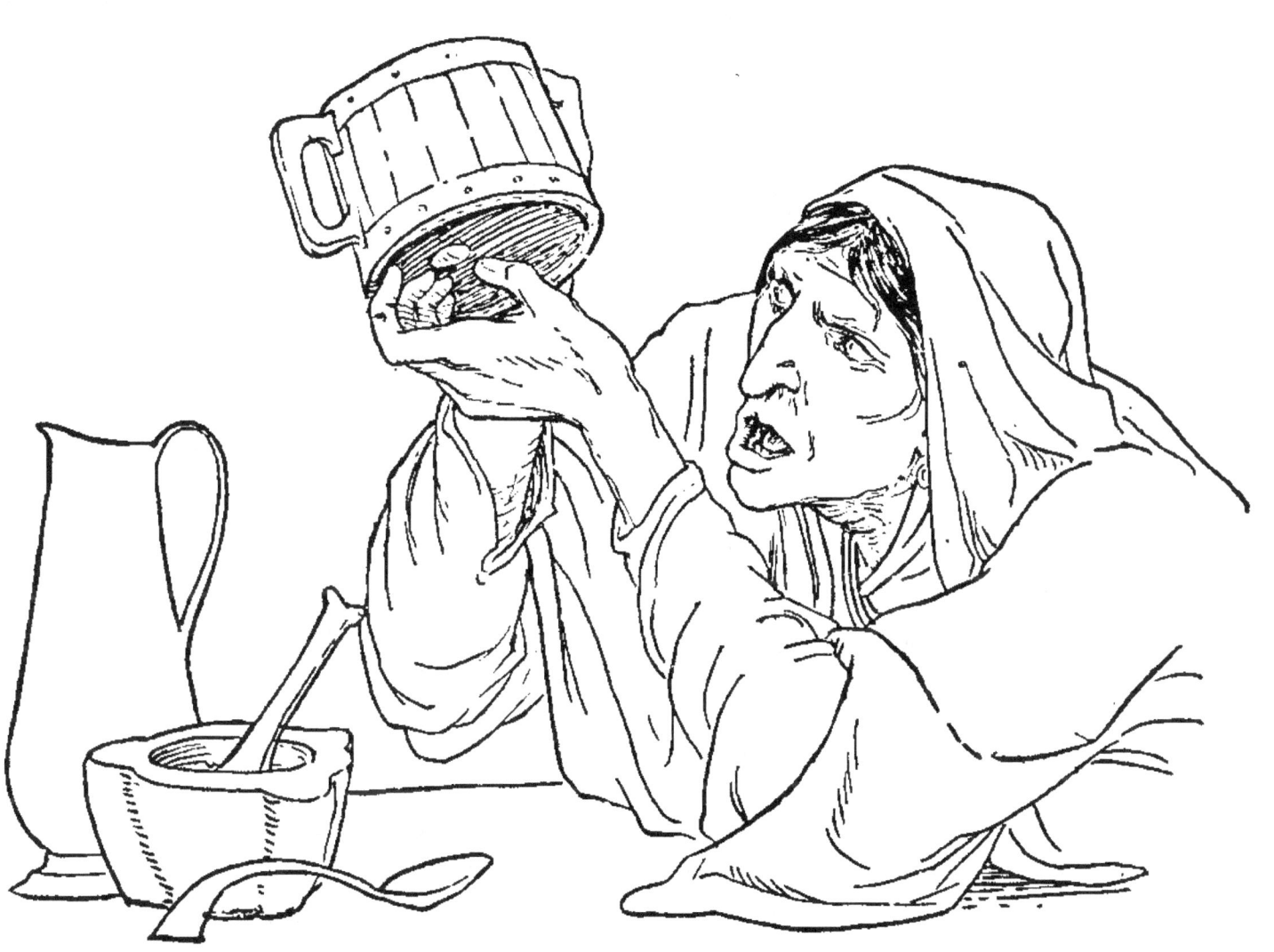

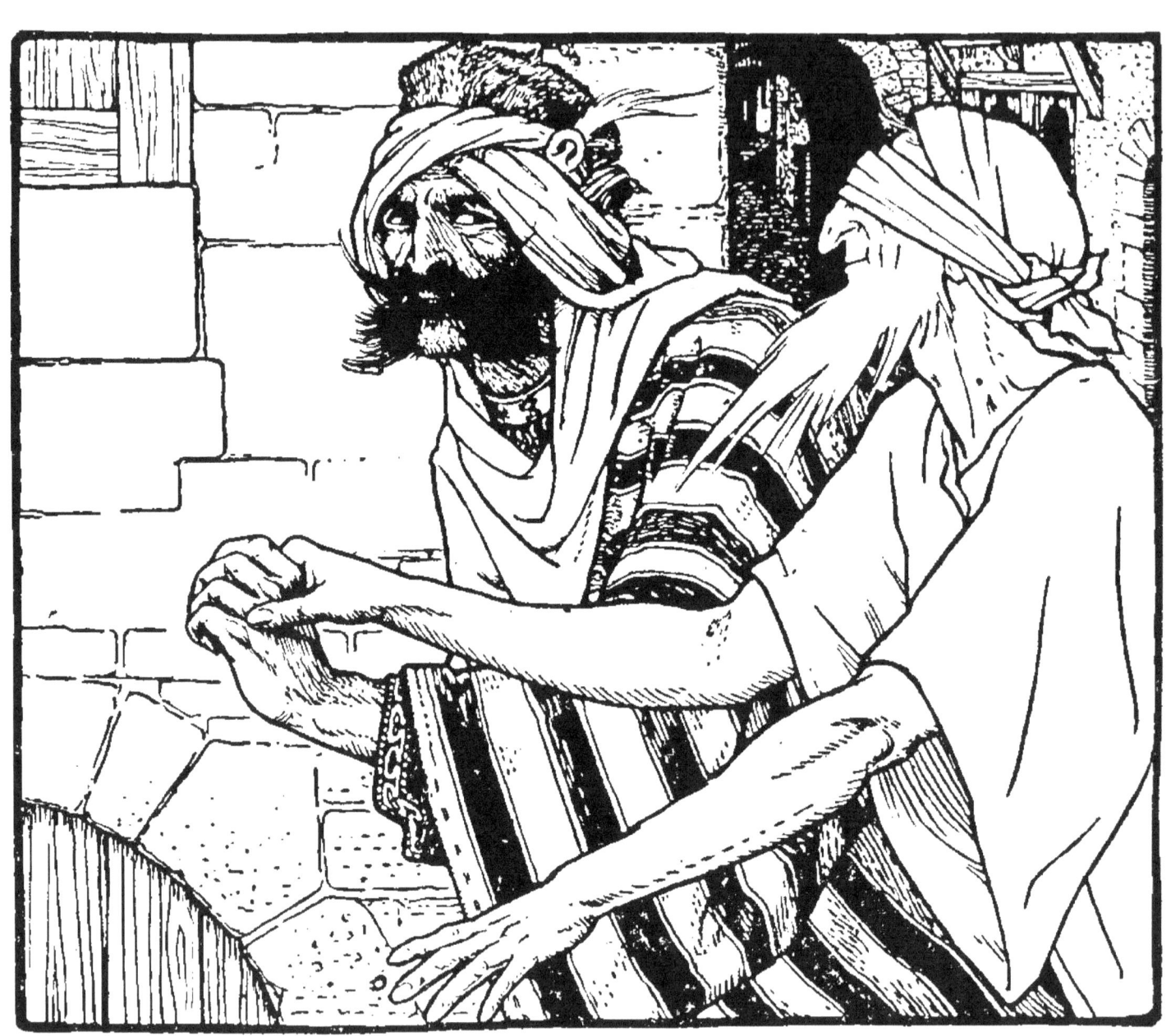

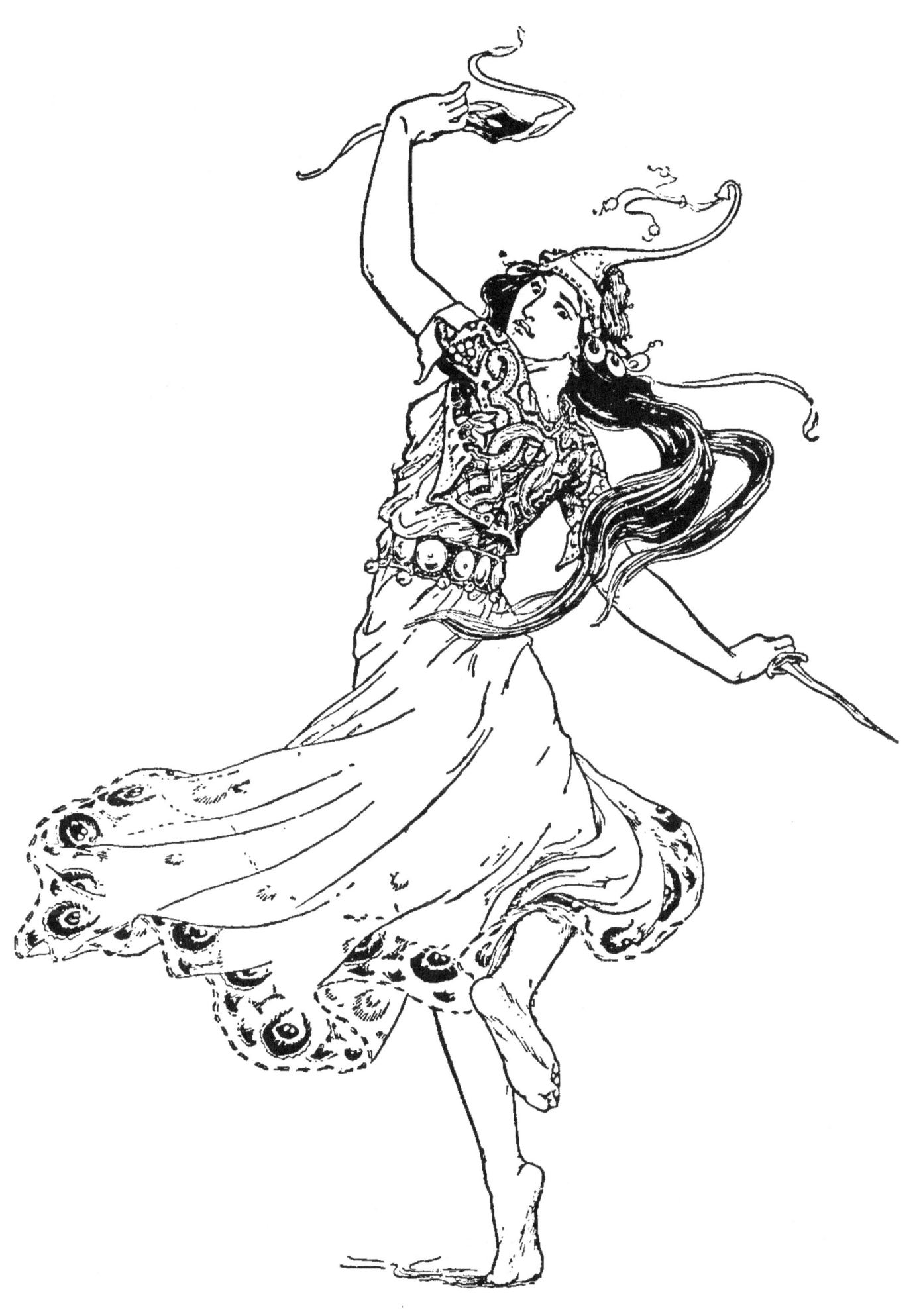

MORGIANA DANCING

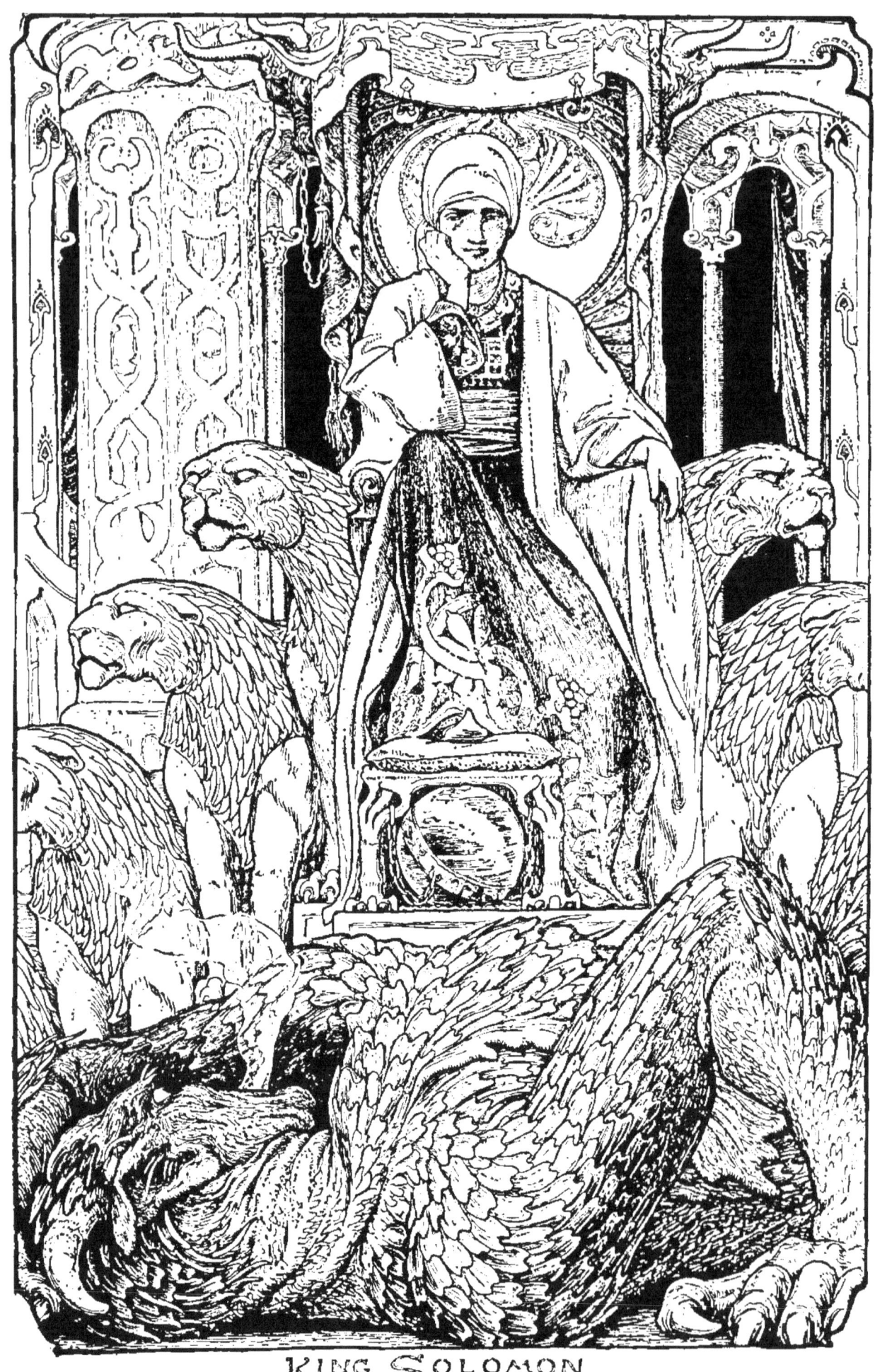

KING SOLOMON
AND THE REBELLIOUS GENIE

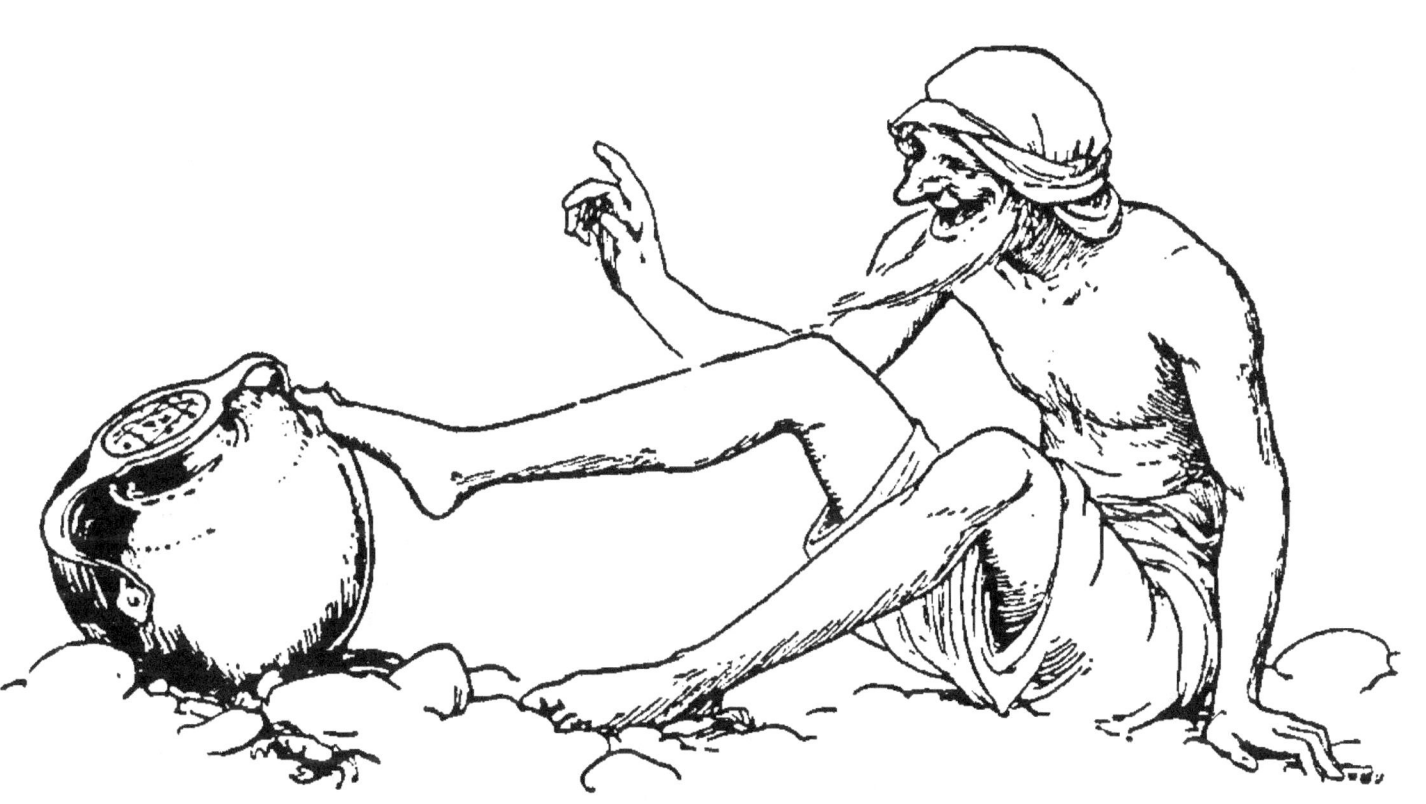

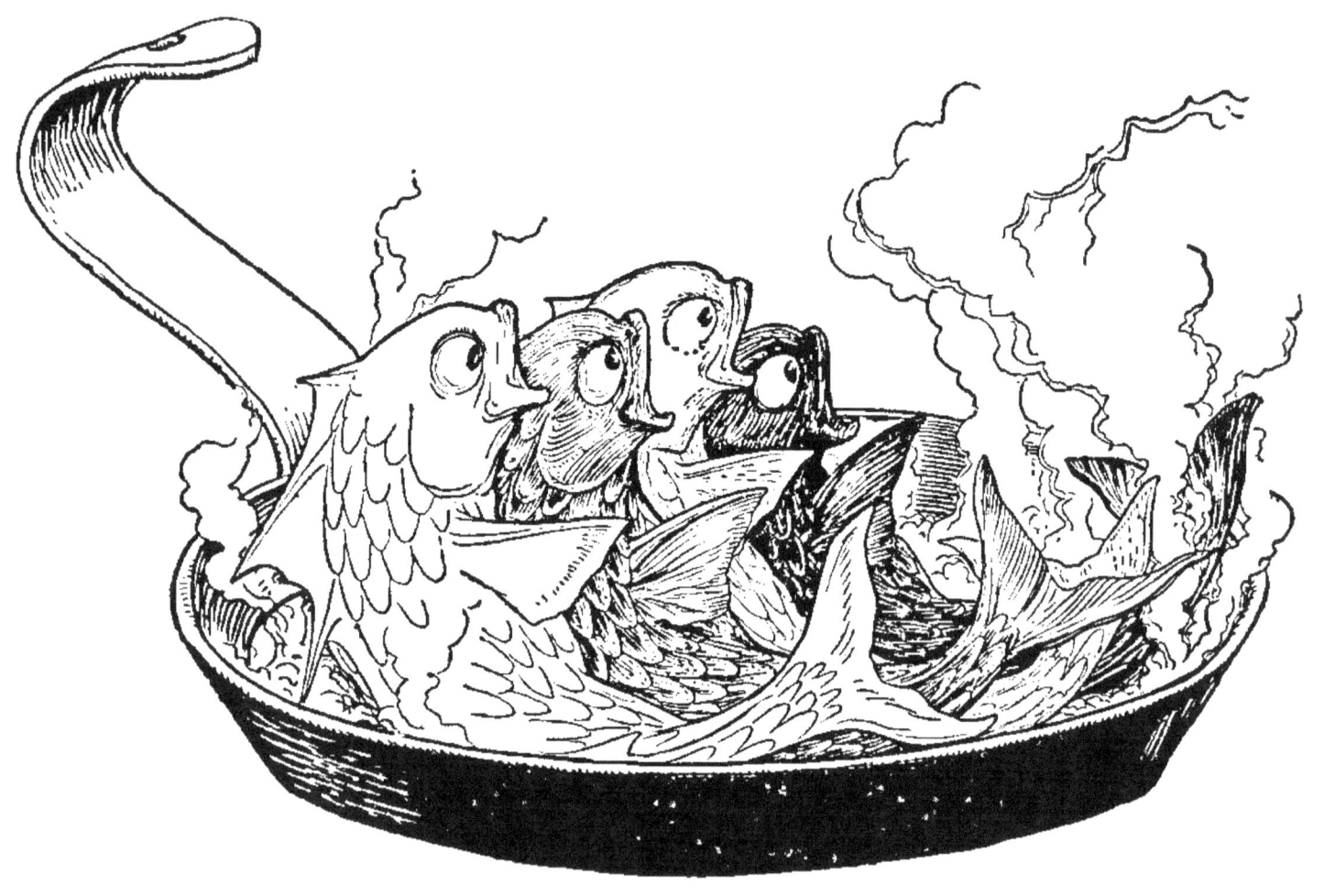

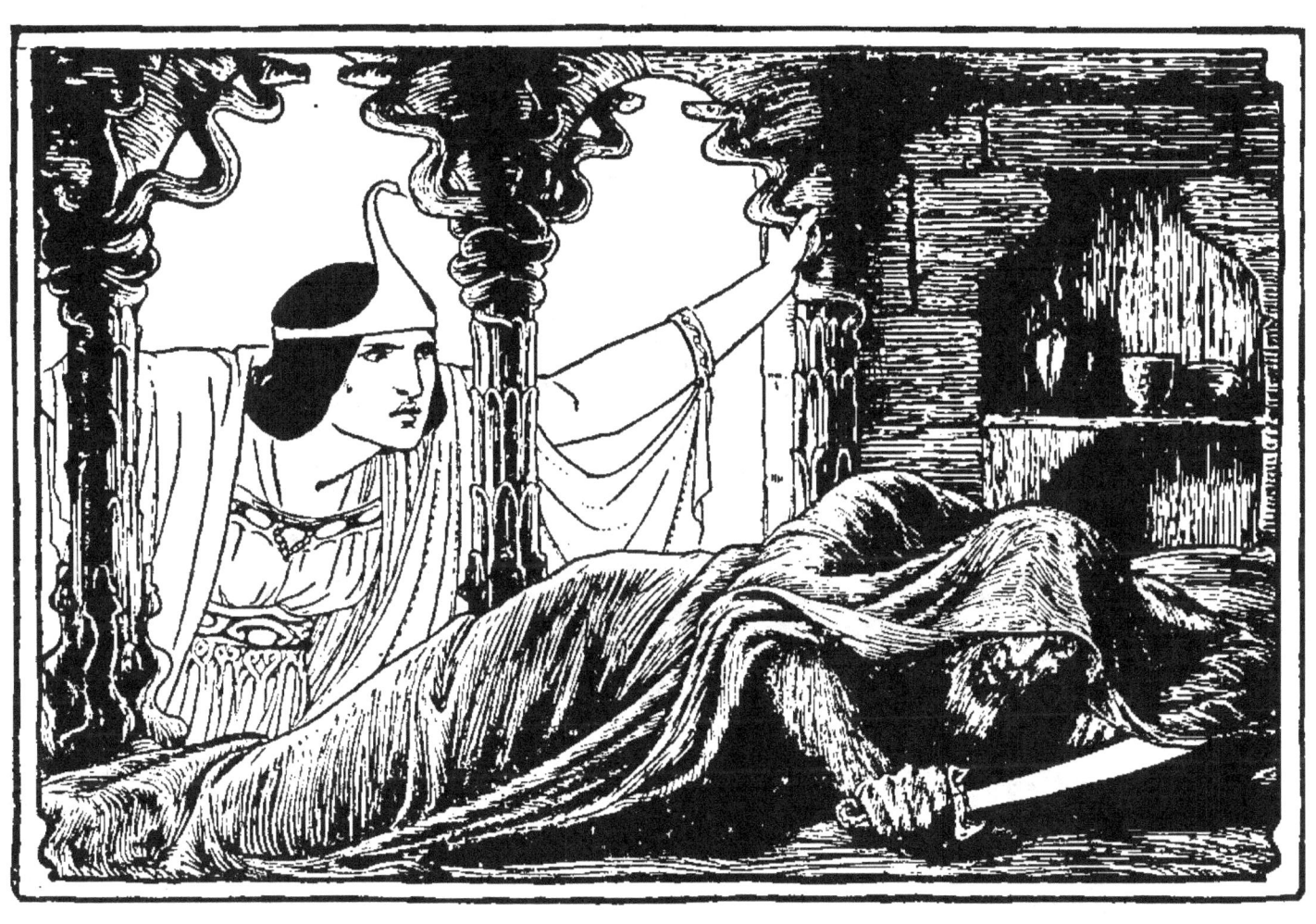

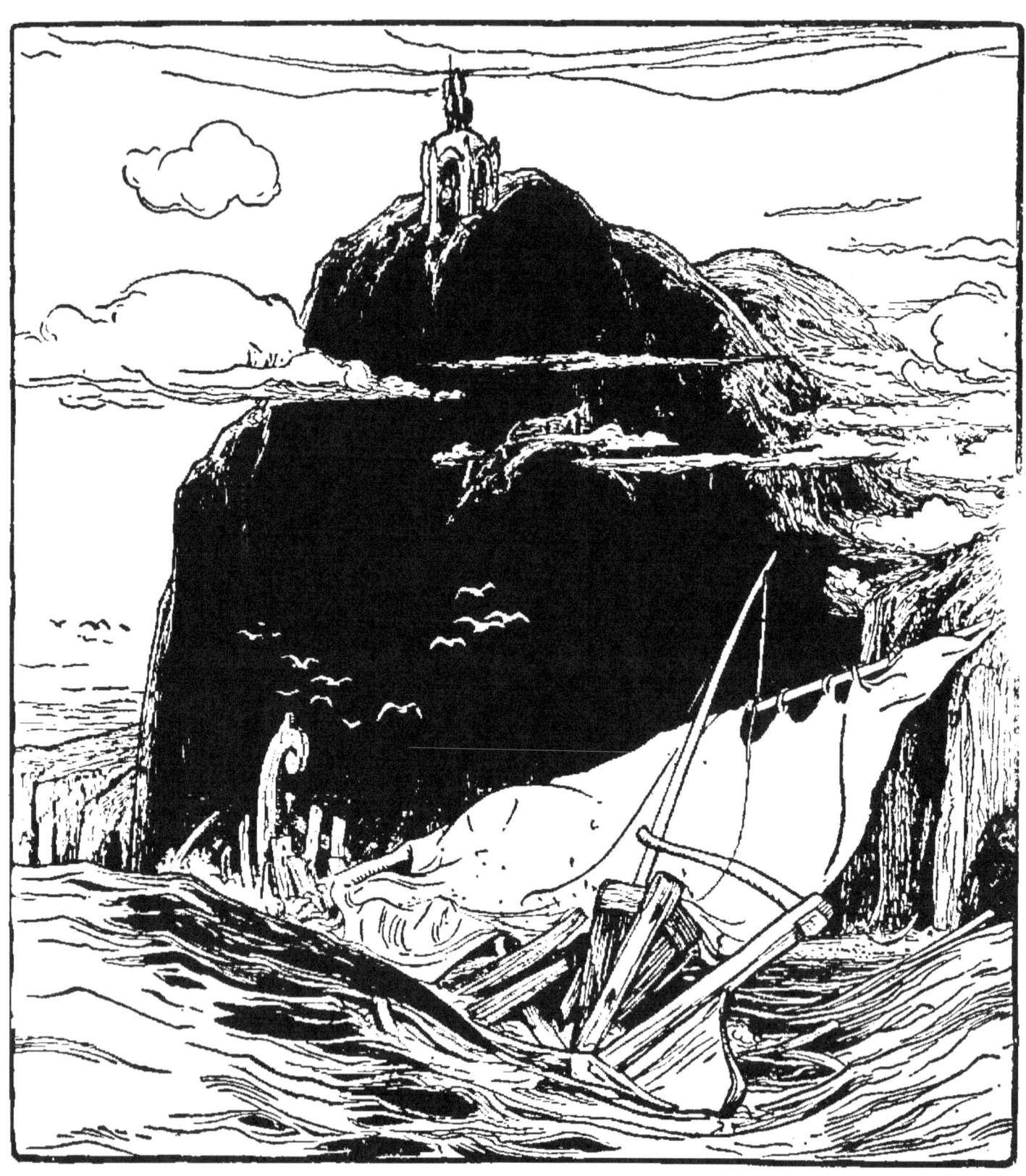

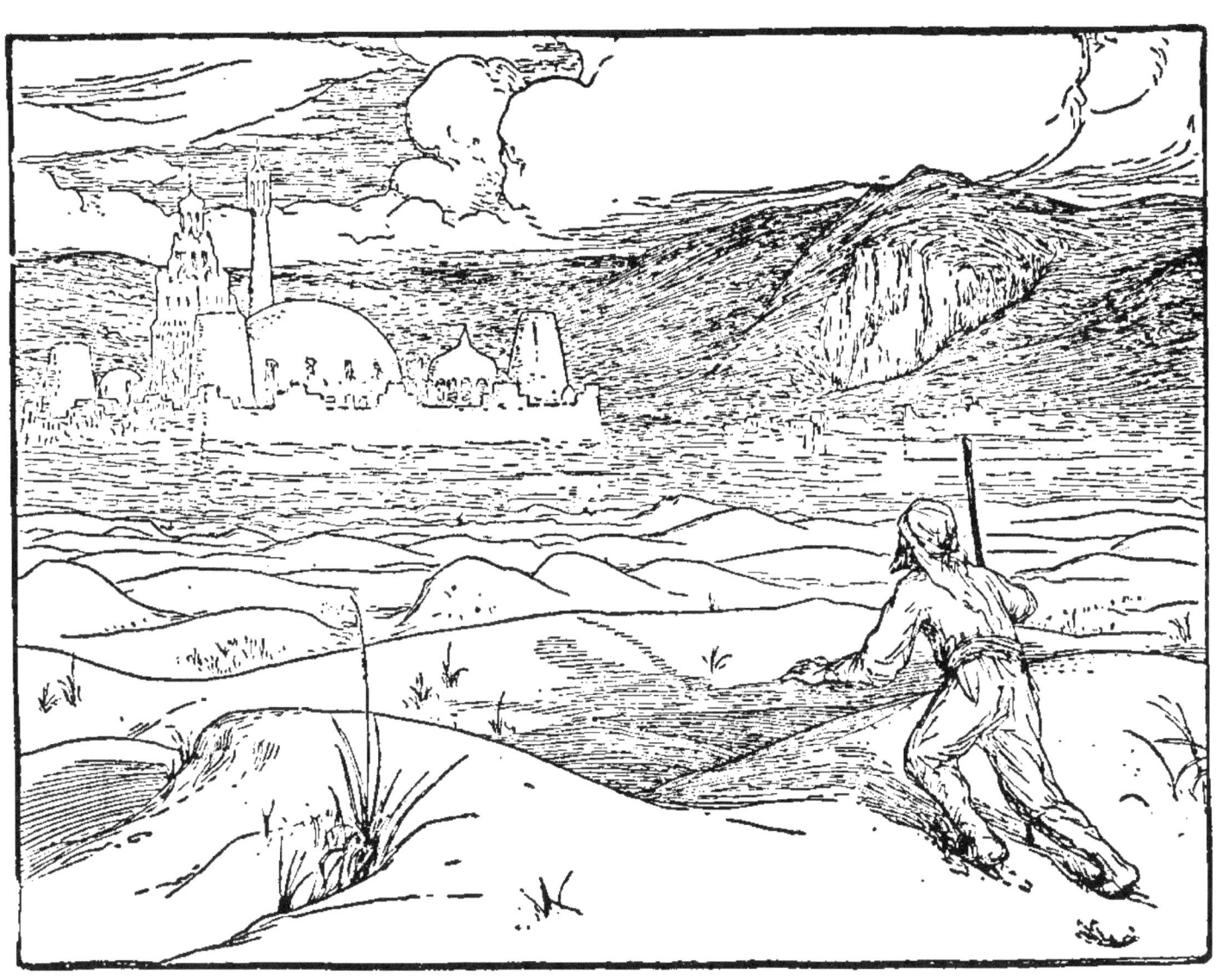

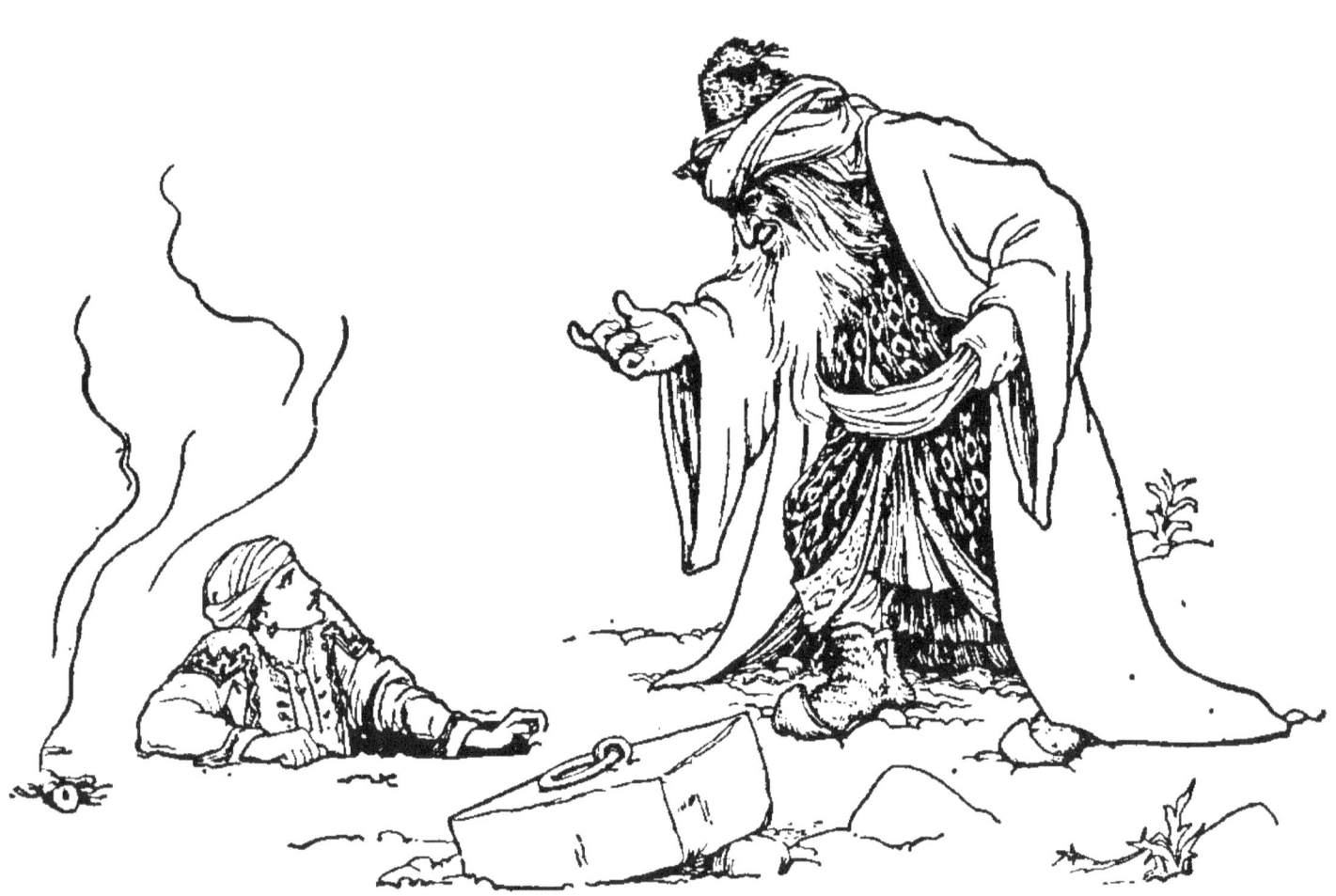

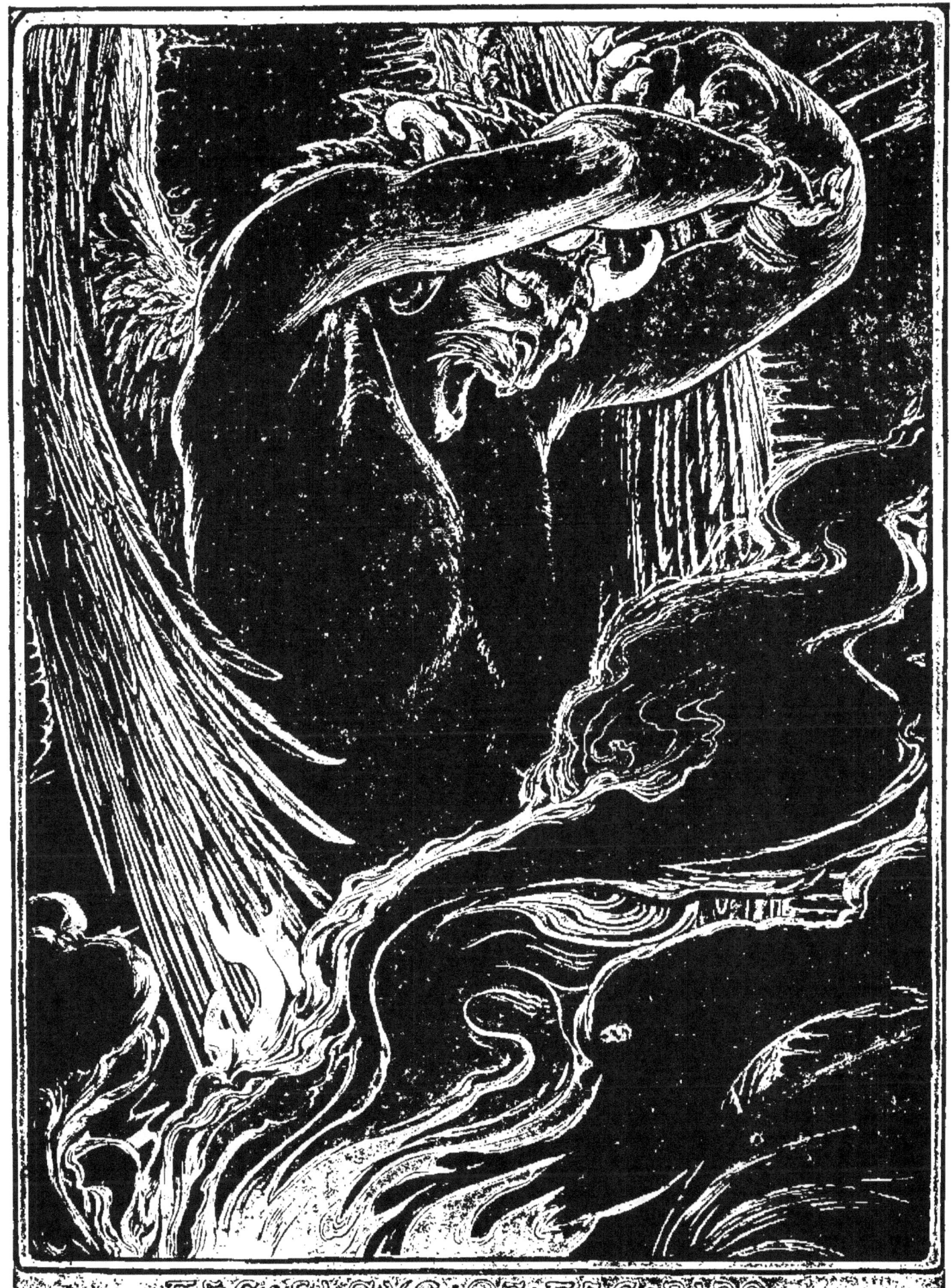

THE·SLAVE·OF·THE·RING

The genie carries the bride and bridegroom to Aladdin's house

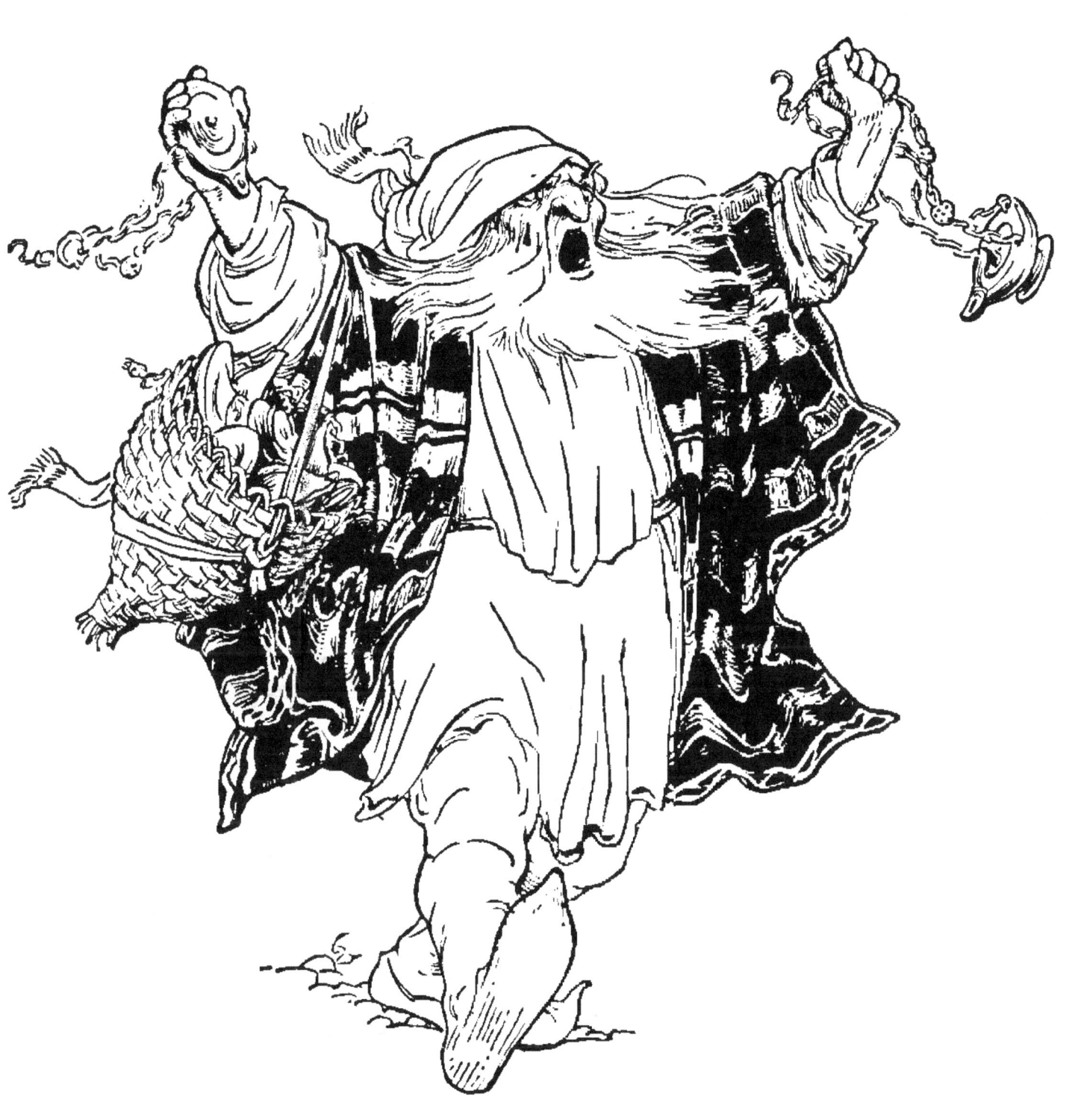

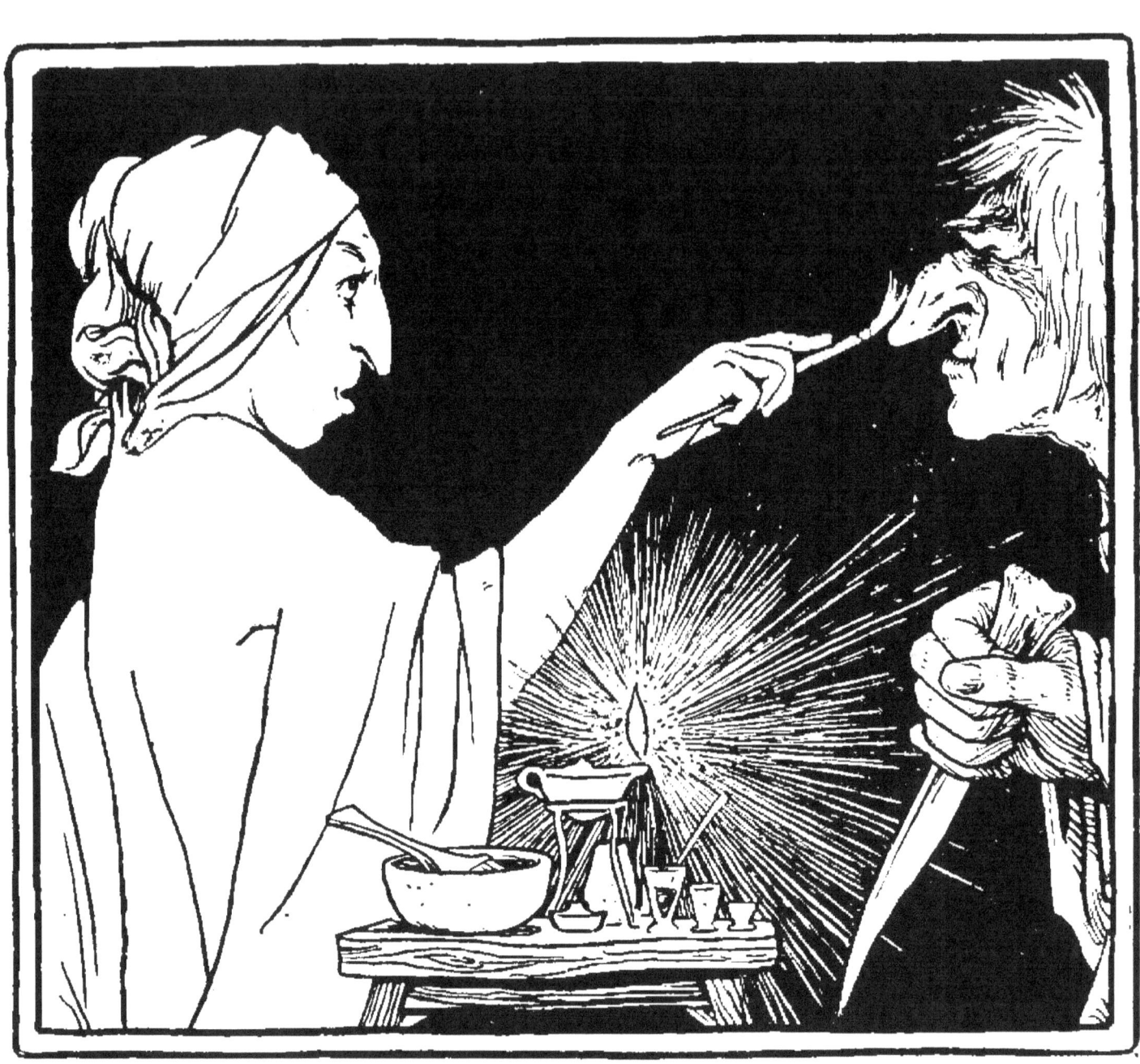

www.ingramcontent.com/pod-product-compliance
Lightning Source LLC
Chambersburg PA
CBHW081622220526
45468CB00010B/2990